FOREST REGENERATION IN ONTARIO

UNIVERSITY OF TORONTO
FORESTRY BULLETIN, NO. 2

Forest Regeneration in Ontario

BASED ON A REVIEW OF SURVEYS
CONDUCTED IN THE PROVINCE
DURING THE PERIOD 1918–1951

By R. C. HOSIE

Published for THE RESEARCH COUNCIL OF ONTARIO
By UNIVERSITY OF TORONTO PRESS: 1953

Foreword

THE renewability of the forest is an important factor affecting our long-term economy, as it provides the basis for the sustained or continuous yield of forest products from land best suited to this crop. Success in forest management depends primarily on the establishment of adequate regeneration of desirable species as soon as possible after the mature forest is cut. It is therefore important in preparing to implement a sustained-yield management policy to know how well this requirement is being met under present operating conditions, and it was with the object of having a comprehensive statement on the situation in Ontario that the Research Council of Ontario requested Professor Hosie to review and report on the regeneration surveys that had been undertaken by various government and industrial agencies in this Province.

From Professor Hosie's report it is apparent that a great deal of work has been done and much useful information obtained with respect to this problem; but it must also be evident that the results of these surveys would have been of even greater value if there had been more uniformity in their design and undertaking and a closer co-ordination among the groups concerned.

In parts of eastern Canada, particularly those influenced by an oceanic climate, natural regeneration of the forest is generally considered to be satisfactory. Some readers may feel that this is also true for Ontario, especially when consideration is given to the extent of forest land in this Province and the progress that is being made in the chemical utilization of tree species previously considered to be worthless. However this situation is less satisfactory when we remember the variation that exists both in the quality and in the usefulness of tree species for different purposes and in the productive capacity of forest soils. The evidence presented in this report shows that it is the more valuable species and those in greatest demand at the present time that have the poorest regeneration, and that it is often on the better growing sites that restocking is inadequate. If we are to depend for our future supplies of forest products mainly on second growth stands that are either poorly stocked, and often with inferior species, or fully stocked but growing on the poorer sites, then the competitive position of the wood-using industries of the Province will tend to deteriorate.

v

One important objective of forest management is to make as efficient use of the productive capacity of the forest soil as possible. It has been stated authoritatively that on many of our better growing sites in eastern Canada the forest yield may be doubled under proper management. The first step towards this objective is to ensure that the regeneration after harvesting is adequate. Professor Hosie's report is of importance in assisting us to evaluate the present situation in this regard for Ontario and in providing those interested in the techniques of regeneration surveys with a critical assessment of the work that has been done in this Province.

J. W. B. Sisam

Preface

THIS review of forest regeneration surveys has been sponsored and supported by the Research Council of Ontario. The Advisory Committee on Forestry Research of the Council in 1948 approved the recommendation submitted by its Sub-committee on Forest Biology "that a review be made of information presently available from regeneration surveys as carried out by all agencies within the Province." Work on the review was commenced by the writer in the summer of 1949.

Through the courtesy of the Ontario Forest Industries Association, the Ontario Department of Lands and Forests, the Forestry Branch of Canada, and the pulp and paper companies and lumber companies in Ontario, reports, and data where no reports were available, of all regeneration surveys completed by government and private agencies within the province were obtained. These were analysed, as they were received, with the assistance of Mr. F. G. Jackson in 1949 and Mr. J. A. C. Grant in 1950, both at the time members of the Faculty of Forestry, University of Toronto. The abstracts of the survey reports which form the second part of this bulletin are therefore, in the majority of cases, a compilation of three independent reviews. They have been submitted for approval to the agencies responsible for the original reports in order to ensure accurate tabulating of the results of the surveys. In the abstracts of Part II square brackets have been used to indicate my comment on the content of the reports.

With the co-operation of the woodlands departments of the pulp and paper companies in Ontario and the two government forest services, field observations were made by the writer during the summer months of 1949, 1950, and 1951 on the timber limits of all the companies for which forest regeneration surveys have been reported, on areas where surveys have been conducted by government forest services, and on areas in different parts of the Province where surveys have not been made. These observations have been invaluable in the analysis and appraisal of the survey data.

The reports and all data received have been placed in the library of the Faculty of Forestry, University of Toronto, and will be retained there for purposes of reference.

R. C. H.

Toronto, Ontario
January, 1953

Contents

PART I

PART II

ABSTRACTS OF REPORTS, 1919–1951

Illustrations

Introduction

FOREST regeneration surveys were started in Ontario in 1919 under the direction of the Commission of Conservation. The first one was carried out in an area of the pulpwood forest, about forty miles west of Iroquois Falls, on the limits of the Abitibi Power and Paper Company and in co-operation with that Company. It was for the purpose of determining the rate of growth and the extent and character of the reproduction of balsam fir and spruce in the virgin forest, and the relationship between this growth and reproduction and that on cut-over land.

In the report of that survey there are two important statements regarding the reproduction: first, "There is considerably less spruce and balsam on the cut-over areas than in the uncut forest"; and second, "That on the cut-over areas there is a low spruce content compared to that of balsam." (See p. 38.)

In 1920 the Commission directed a second survey on the limits of the Spanish River Pulp and Paper Mills, in co-operation with that company. The survey was for the purpose of determining the influence of cutting on growth and regeneration of pulpwood species. With regard to the latter, it is stated in the conclusions of the report that "the present young growth [referring to spruce and balsam] was nearly all present as advance growth at the time of cutting." (See p. 39.)

The first of these reports expresses doubt regarding the future of spruce on cut-over pulpwood areas, and the second suggests the probability that the future spruce and balsam cut will develop from reproduction that was established in the old stand previous to cutting.

In 1921 the forestry activities of the Commission of Conservation were taken over by the Dominion Forest Service. During the next few years two additional surveys were completed by the federal service in Ontario, one in Algonquin Park and the other in the Sudbury District.

A review of these early surveys, and of similar studies conducted in other parts of Canada by the federal service up to 1936, was published by the Dominion Forest Service in 1938. (See p. 46.) The conclusions given in that review were optimistic regarding the general nature of reproduction on cut-over areas in Canada, though doubt was expressed concerning the future of white and red pine in Ontario. However some reservations were made regarding the reliability of the conclusions in the review. In the words of the author, "While the surveys indicate in a general way that regeneration in disturbed forests is most satisfactory, an analysis of the work undertaken indicates that such results should be treated with some caution at this stage of the investigation."

At the time of the publication of that review the Ontario Forestry Branch had completed several regeneration surveys in different parts of the Province, work on which had been started in 1930. The Spruce Falls Power and Paper Company had also completed preliminary surveys on cut-over land in the Kapuskasing area which had been started in 1933. The results of the surveys of these two agencies were not such as to encourage optimism regarding the nature of the reproduction on cut-over land in the areas examined. Thus uncertainty regarding the real nature of reproduction on cut-over areas increased.

Following this period the Ontario Forestry Branch temporarily discontinued forest research activities while undergoing a reorganization which resulted in its separation into a number of divisions within the Department of Lands and Forests, and the dropping, about 1941, of the title "Forestry Branch." Also, depression conditions preceding the Second World War curtailed the research work of practically all other forest agencies. It was not until after the war that the greatest effort was made to remove the uncertainty that had arisen and to decide if possible whether or not the reproduction on cut-over forest areas could be considered satisfactory.

The newly organized Research Division of the Department of Lands and Forests completed ten surveys during the years 1946–51. In the same period the Forestry Branch of Canada completed a three-year survey for all of Canada east of the Rockies. The majority of the larger pulp and paper companies that had not been active in this work previous to 1946 began regeneration studies, some of them in cooperation with the government forest services. The companies that had previously carried out surveys increased their efforts, so that at the present date fifty-seven surveys have been completed in Ontario.

This review of these surveys is submitted in two parts. The first part presents a general view of the nature of tree reproduction on cut-over forest land in the Province, followed by an analysis of the procedure used in conducting and reporting regeneration surveys and by a statement of conclusions and recommendations. In the second part the abstracts of the surveys reviewed are arranged chronologically under the names of the agencies responsible for the original reports.

Part I

THE PROBABLE NATURE AND EXTENT
OF FOREST REGENERATION IN THE PROVINCE

THE reports of regeneration surveys for which there are abstracts in the second part of this review provide the basis for the views given here. These reports contain a great deal of information about the species of the northern pulpwood area. Over a quarter of a million samples have been examined for the presence or absence of spruce and balsam alone. For the other commercial species a relatively smaller number of observations have been made and the majority of these during surveys that were conducted in the more southerly part of the commercial forest area and previous to the introduction of the surveying methods that are in use at the present time. Of the species other than spruce and balsam, white pine has received the most attention and a fairly clear picture of it can be obtained.

The surveys of the Department of Lands and Forests carried out in the North Bay (No. 3)[1] and Algonquin Park (No. 6) areas reveal that in general good white pine reproduction does not occur following logging operations. However when it does occur, it is usually found in the greatest numbers on the poorest sites and invariably following logging operations that have coincided with seed years. This finding has been substantiated by personal studies and observations made in the valley of the Little Nipissing River on the timber limits of the Gillies Brothers Lumber Company (Figs. 2 and 3), where there is at present a young stand of white pine that seeded in over parts of an area where cutting occurred immediately before and at the time of a good seed year. Elsewhere reproduction did not occur or was sparse.

A seed supply, however, is only one of the essentials for good natural reproduction of white pine. The seedbed is equally important as is also, in many instances, shelter for the seedlings during the first few years after germination. The reports referred to above and those of other surveys indicate that one or other of these two requirements is often so unsatisfactorily met following logging that reproduction does not occur even where seed drifts in from adjacent areas. In the words of Brodie (No. 8): "The evidence seems to be quite consistent, we cannot log clear in white pine stands and get regeneration unless some accident such as fire has set up suitable conditions. Forest fires have

[1]The number in brackets refers to the number given the relevant abstract in Part II of this report.

accidentally in some instances set up conditions which have given pine regeneration, but that fires do not usually have this effect is readily demonstrated,—other factors are involved."

The situation with regard to the regeneration of red pine following logging is somewhat similar to that for white pine. Candy (No. 10), writing with reference to the Great Lakes–St. Lawrence Region, states: "Considering white and red pine only, there are only 74 stems per acre on areas disturbed by logging and 31 stems per acre on areas disturbed by logging and fire. This low content confirms data derived from the stocked quadrat basis, where these two valuable species were recorded as only 1 to 4 per cent stocked."

The first of the two quotations given above is from an early report of the survey work of the Ontario Department of Lands and Forests, 1930–3, and the second from a recent report of the survey conducted by the Forestry Branch of Canada, 1946–8. They indicate clearly the unfavourable situation with regard to the regeneration of both white and red pine following conventional logging.

Jack pine regeneration following conventional logging has been in the past generally unsatisfactory (Fig. 4). What the results will be following mechanized logging is not yet known. There is evidence that the use of mechanical equipment in logging greatly disturbs the litter and exposes more mineral soil than does manual and horse logging. This may be effective in increasing the amount of regeneration. Certain cultural measures to be applied at the time of logging, such as brush scattering and scarification, are at present being tried experimentally by certain companies with the co-operation in some cases of one or other of the two government services. However, as these tests are still in the initial stage it is difficult to draw any definite conclusions regarding the effectiveness or the practicability of such measures.

For yellow birch, studies have been started by the Research Division of the Department of Lands and Forests and as part of the research work of the Faculty of Forestry of the University of Toronto, but no reports have been issued. From personal observations made on cut-over areas in Algonquin Park and in the forest area south of the park boundary, the outlook appears less favourable than for white, red, or jack pine.

For the other tolerant hardwoods there is no information.

The intolerant hardwoods, poplar and white birch, have received some attention in most of the surveys conducted in the pulpwood region and there is general agreement that they are species that reproduce without difficulty by means of root suckers and coppice growth, respectively (Fig. 7).

For spruce and balsam the situation as revealed in different reports is somewhat confused, largely because investigators have applied the stocked quadrat method in various ways and have interpreted the data differently. For the most part, however, concern is expressed for the future of spruce on the better sites while the regeneration of balsam is considered to be generally good.

To permit a comparison of the results obtained for these two species, stocking percentages recorded by nine investigators in twenty areas are given in Table I. These have been changed where necessary to percentages that would have been recorded had each used a quadrat size of 1/1000 acre. The revised stocking percentages as shown in the table were obtained in all cases but one by combining the stocking percentages recorded for the area worked in regardless of the types

TABLE I

PERCENTAGE OF 1/1000 ACRE QUADRATS STOCKED TO SPRUCE AND BALSAM
FOR AREAS SURVEYED BY DIFFERENT INVESTIGATORS
(BASED ON 75,341 QUADRATS)

Location of area	Investigator	Years since cut	Types	No. of quadrats	Percentage stocked to spruce	Percentage stocked to balsam	Percentage stocked to spruce or balsam
Valora	Larsson	1–5	all	3902	27	44	62
Valora (English R.)	Henderson	1–5	all	705	28	38	63
English R.	Cameron	1–5	all	1849	29	44	63
Lac des Milles Lacs	Larsson	1–5	all	1690	27	19	42
"	"	6–15	all	2393	45	47	77
"	McKay	1–5	BSS*	929	44	8	50
Black Sturgeon	Larsson	1–5	all	1041	19	48	56
"	"	6–10	all	5301	17	45	53
"	Kagetsu	5–10	all	8709	17	47	55
"	Abbott	1–5	all	2750	20	39	51
Lake Nipigon	Larsson	1–5	all	433	48	35	71
"	"	6–10	all	3063	20	53	65
Longlac	"	1–5	all	346	26	25	42
"	"	6–10	all	356	25	25	39
Marathon	"	1–5	slopes	571	22	51	59
"	"	6–10	all	6102	19	30	41
Kapuskasing	Bonner	20	all	4440	47	56	77
"	Hosie	1–5	all	1370	36	41	63
"	"	13–16	all	2511	41	42	71
Cochrane	Candy	6–21+	all	27,880	47	49	79

*BSS—Black spruce swamp.

encountered.[2] The basic work involved in computing the new percentages was done by J. A. C. Grant.[3]

The twenty areas selected form a representative sample area for the Province (see Fig. 1) and the men responsible for the data given in the table are a fair selection of the investigators in the organizations that have conducted regeneration surveys, there being six from the forest industries and one each from the provincial forest service, the federal forest service, and the university.

By applying the stocking standards of the Forestry Branch of Canada (described on page 19), one may make the following three observations:

1. *Fourteen* of the *twenty* areas surveyed are understocked to spruce with the other *six* moderately stocked. *Seven* of the understocked areas are a failure or are very close to it.

2. *Eight* of the *twenty* areas are understocked to balsam with the other *twelve* moderately stocked. *Two* of the understocked areas are a failure.

3. For spruce or balsam, *ten* of the areas are well stocked, *nine* are moderately stocked, and *one* is understocked. *Three* of the moderately stocked areas are very close to being understocked.

These observations are based on an arbitrary standard which may be too high. If we lower it a few points then the number of understocked areas and of those declared failures will not be as great and the impression obtained will undoubtedly be more favourable. Moreover the percentages in the table, with the exception that has been noted, are averages of a number of different types. When the stocking percentages for each type are shown (Table II) it will be seen that there are types that should not be included when certain areas are classed as failures. For example: the stocking percentage for spruce obtained by Kagetsu in the Black Sturgeon area is 17 (Table I). For the five types that he encountered the stocking percentages range from 11 in the hardwood type to 34 in the black spruce swamp type (Table II). All of the area that he examined should not therefore be classed as a failure for spruce. Other similar examples can be found by referring to the two tables.

Thus the stocking of spruce or of balsam within any area varies with the type of forest. For spruce it is considerably higher in the black spruce swamp type than on any of the better drained sites. For

[2]The exception refers to the Lac des Milles Lacs area surveyed by McKay where all plots were apparently taken in the black spruce swamp type.

[3]See his bulletin *The Relationship between Stocking and Size of Quadrat* (Toronto: University of Toronto Press, 1952).

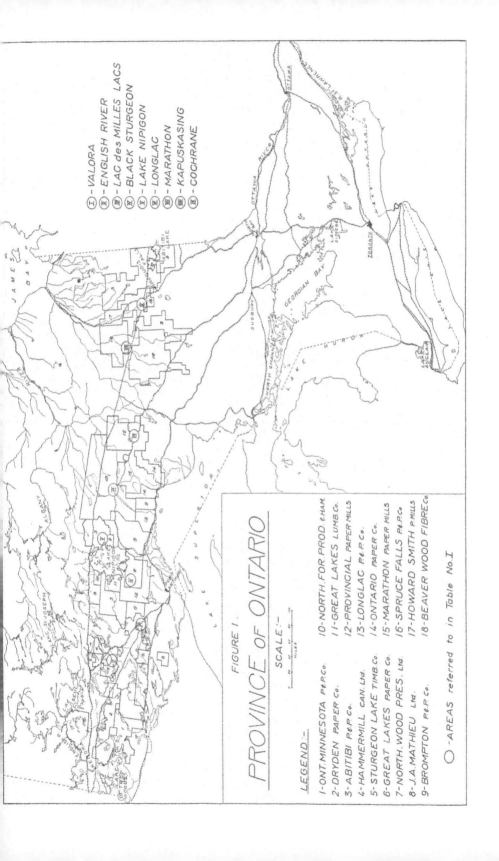

FIGURE 1.

PROVINCE of ONTARIO

SCALE:-

LEGEND:-

1-ONT.MINNESOTA P&P.Co.
2-DRYDEN PAPER Co.
3-ABITIBI P&P.Co.
4-HAMMERMILL CAN.Ltd.
5-STURGEON LAKE TIMB Co.
6-GREAT LAKES PAPER Co.
7-NORTH.WOOD PRES. Ltd.
8-J.A.MATHIEU Ltd.
9-BROMPTON P&P.Co.

10-NORTH.FOR.PROD &.HAM.
11-GREAT LAKES LUMB.Co.
12-PROVINCIAL PAPER MILLS
13-LONGLAC P&P.Co.
14-ONTARIO PAPER Co.
15-MARATHON PAPER MILLS
16-SPRUCE FALLS P&P.Co.
17-HOWARD SMITH P.MILLS
18-BEAVER WOOD FIBRE Co.

○ -AREAS referred to in Table No.I

Ⓘ - VALORA
Ⓘ - ENGLISH RIVER
Ⓘ - LAC des MILLES LACS
Ⓘ - BLACK STURGEON
Ⓘ - LAKE NIPIGON
Ⓘ - LONGLAC
Ⓘ - MARATHON
Ⓘ - KAPUSKASING
Ⓘ - COCHRANE

TABLE II

PERCENTAGE OF 1/1000 ACRE QUADRATS STOCKED TO SPRUCE AND BALSAM FOR DIFFERENT TYPES AS REPORTED BY DIFFERENT INVESTIGATORS

Investigator	No. of quadrats	BS	BSS	S	MS	M	H
Percentages stocked to Spruce							
Kagetsu	8709		34	13	28	13	11
Henderson	705		46	20		13	
Abbott	2750		30	15	17	17	
Cameron	1849		50	21		15	
Larsson	1041		26	26	20	17	
Candy	27,880	72		46		22	
Bonner	4440	43		38		22	
Hosie	1370	43	50	27		20	
McKay	929		44				
Percentages stocked to Balsam							
Kagetsu	8709		18	61	67	50	36
Henderson	705		25	51		73	
Abbott	2750		20	51	38	47	
Cameron	1849		21	50		61	
Larsson	1041	24		59	55	44	
Candy	27,880	24		55		68	
Bonner	4440	57		59		51	
Hosie	1370	23	25	65		71	
McKay	929		8				

BS—Black spruce flat; BSS—Black spruce swamp; S—Softwood, mainly spruce–balsam slope; MS—Mixed softwood, mainly jack pine crown types; M—Mixed softwood–hardwood; H—Hardwood.

balsam the reverse is true, the higher stocking occurring on the relatively dry sites.

It follows, then, that within any area surveyed, if the majority of the quadrats examined are situated on the better drained soils the average stocking obtained for spruce will be relatively low. The low average stocking percentages for spruce shown in Table I are, in part at least, explained by the fact that most of the work done in each of the areas where several types were examined was in types other than the black spruce swamps.

With the additional data of Table II the probability of a wrong interpretation of the survey results is greatly reduced, although not entirely removed. There is still some uncertainty regarding the types. For example, few of the investigators have recognized the black spruce flat (Fig. 9) and any recordings made in that type are doubtless included in the percentage given for one or more of the other types. Candy does not give percentages for the black spruce swamp (Fig. 8) and the mixed softwood types (Figs. 10, 11) though no doubt the data for these were included in the figures for the softwood or the black spruce flat or both; this may partly explain the high averages of 46 and 72 shown in Table II. The stocking percentage obtained by Bonner for the black spruce swamp was omitted, as too few samples had been obtained in that type to warrant its inclusion.

Although it cannot be said definitely that all nine investigators are referring to entirely similar conditions for any one of the six types referred to in Table II, there is for some of them, as for example the S, MS, and M, which are the slope or upland types, sufficient evidence for us to accept the following as being approximately correct with regard to spruce: in the softwood type the stocking percentages range from 13 to 46,[4] in the mixed softwood from 17 to 28, and in the mixed-wood from 13 to 22; on the basis of present standards it can be stated further that two of the investigators found the softwood type a failure, one the mixed softwood, and five the mixedwood.

Keeping in mind that we have no recognized standard, that the percentages given are averages, and that there may have been error with respect to the types, the following conclusion may be reached with regard to spruce:

In view of the relatively large number of areas shown in Table I to have low average stocking for spruce on all types examined, except the black spruce swamp (Table II), certain parts of cut-over areas in these types are very poorly stocked to that species with the probability that some parts are unstocked (Figs. 12–19).

Since none of the reports indicate the percentage of cut-over forest land that is not reproducing to spruce there is no exact way of determining what that area may be. There is, however, evidence that it would include portions of the forest area within all of the forest types, except the black spruce swamp. It is within these types that some of the best spruce sites occur; therefore it is the most valuable portion of the forest land that is involved.

As to the probability of these poorly stocked areas improving as a result of later seeding-in, the evidence is conflicting. Approximately half of the investigators claim that practically all of the spruce regeneration on well-drained sites is advance growth,[5] while others claim that a good deal of seeding-in takes place even twenty years after cutting. Some have shown increasing stocking with age of cutover. Others point out that this increase may be the result of earlier cuttings having been considerably lighter than later ones. Several refer to the poor condition of the seedbed and state that there is abundance of

---

[4]The percentage 46 (Candy) is doubtless higher than would be the case if it had been possible to define clearly all the types.

[5]Young trees that have become established before cutting operations are begun.

seed but few suitable places for the establishment of seedlings. Actually there is no factual evidence in the reports for such statements, which are based mainly on observations that, in some cases at least, have been influenced by the faulty determination of seedlings, advance growth (Figs. 6, 7), and perhaps also layerings (Figs. 11, 12).[6]

Turning now to an appraisal of the regeneration of balsam, one finds the picture somewhat clearer. The stocking percentages given in Table II for that species, on the three types S, MS, and M, are higher than those for spruce and none of them suggest failure on the basis of present stocking standards. It is clear, then, that the regeneration of balsam is considerably better on the cut-over areas in the types referred to than is that of spruce. Just how much better it is, is difficult to say.

These higher percentages obtained for balsam have led some investigators to conclude that when spruce and balsam are considered together, the general situation on pulpwood cut-over areas is satisfactory. It does not follow, however, that all areas having little spruce present will have balsam to compensate for the lack of spruce. There are areas with low stocking for both species.

An average stocking of 65 or 73, or perhaps even 50, may be looked upon by some as indicating a rather good condition. It is difficult, however, to look upon averages below 50 as being satisfactory. But regardless of the value placed on the actual percentages, it is practically certain that the lower the percentage, the more irregular is the stocking on the area and the greater will be the opportunity for parts of it to be without regeneration. Percentages below 50 should be looked upon as indicating irregularity of distribution. Only under exceptional circumstances would that not be the case.

The results of the present study support the following four conclusions regarding spruce and balsam:

1. There are, on some cut-over areas, usually lowland, young stands of spruce that give promise, on the basis of present stocking, of a future cut that may be as good as that harvested.

2. On some other cut-over areas, usually upland, there are numerous young stands of spruce and balsam that give promise on the basis of present stocking of a future cut that may be as good as, or even better than, that harvested.

3. On other cut-over areas the present young growth does not promise, on the basis of present stocking, a future cut of spruce, although it does of spruce and balsam taken together.

[6]A layering is a branch taking root while still attached to and obtaining nourishment from the parent.

4. On still other cut-over areas the present stocking of spruce and balsam is so sparse that it is doubtful that there will be a cut of either of these species when the present stands mature.

The extent of the area in the Province that does not give promise, on the basis of the present reproduction, of a future cut of spruce, or of balsam, or of either species cannot be determined directly from the reports, as the majority of the investigators have not concerned themselves with area directly but have relied solely on stocking percentages within the different types to indicate this. Thus any estimate of what the area of failure may be in the Province has to be based on an evaluation of the acreage of poorly stocked cutover obtained in a few surveys and on an interpretation of the stocking percentages recorded in these and in other surveys carried out in different parts of the cut-over forest.

The reports that give areas of failure in acres, or as percentages of the areas surveyed, are those of the later surveys of the Great Lakes Paper Company and from these have been taken the data given in Table III.

Before using these data, however, it is necessary to point out that, in the determination of the areas of failure, the investigators used a low standard of stocking with the result that acreages and percentages given are probably too high. Also, six of the acreages shown in the table are the writer's estimates based on the recorded number of quadrats given in the reports. These estimates have been made only where acreages were not reported and each is clearly indicated in the table.

The evidence that the conditions found by the Great Lakes Paper Company and given in Table III are typical of those elsewhere in the Province is the degree of equivalence shown when the stocking percentages obtained in the company surveys[7] are compared with those recorded for other areas in the Province (see Table II).

It will be seen in Table III that 15.3 per cent of the total area surveyed was classed as a failure. Also, it may be seen that almost one-third of the area surveyed was in the black spruce swamp type, the one type within which regeneration is usually satisfactory. Therefore if all areas of failure occurred in types other than the black spruce swamps, 22 per cent of the area of these types would be classed a failure. It follows, then, that within the types other than the black spruce swamps the area of failure is greater than 15.3 and probably not much below 22 per cent.

[7]The percentages referred to are those of Abbott, Cameron, Henderson, Kagetsu, and McKay.

TABLE III

AREAS OF FAILURE AS REPORTED IN SURVEYS OF THE
GREAT LAKES PAPER COMPANY

Location	Investi-gator	Area sampled in acres	Acreage of BSS	Acreage of other types	Quadrats in BSS	in all others	Percentage of total area classed as failure	Failure area in acres
Black Sturgeon	Kagetsu	19,800	3050*	16,750*	1492	8052	22.00	4356
Lac des Milles Lacs	McKay	2365	1921	444			11.00	260
Lac des Milles Lacs	McKay (1947)	1165	1165	00			1.90	22
English River	Henderson	1152	539	613			0.00	00
Black Sturgeon	Abbott	2531	670	1861			5.65	143
English River	Cameron	2232	379	1853			3.30	74
Lac des Milles Lacs	Cameron	1907	1367	540			0.63	12
Gull Lake	Cameron	511	341*	170*	649	322	6.50	33
Kashabowie	Cameron	290	249*	41*	471	83	0.00	00
Totals		31,953	9681	22,272				4900

BSS—Black spruce swamp.
*Acreage estimated on the basis of quadrats taken in the BSS type.

Percentage of failure on the total area of 31,953 acres is 15.3.
If failure occurs only in the types other than the BSS, the percentage is 22.

The stocking percentages on which these areas of failure are based were obtained from quadrats of 1/600 acre in size, but the stocking standards used to determine what areas should be classed as failures are those of the Forestry Branch, and their basis is a quadrat size of 1/1000 acre. The result is that the areas classed as failure (below 20 per cent) are actually only those on which stocking percentages below 13[8] would have been obtained had the quadrat size used been 1/1000 acre.

If, on the other hand, the quadrat size had been left at 1/600 acre and the standard used had been brought to the level of that applied by the Forestry Branch, then all areas showing average stocking percentages below 31 would have been classed as failures.

Evidently then, the areas of failure shown in Table III would be considerably increased if the present standards of the Forestry Branch were applied. The percentages would also be more useful if the swamp land could be deleted and the area of failure shown as a percentage

[8]A stocking percentage of 13 based on quadrats of 1/600 acre size is equivalent to one of 20 based on quadrats of 1/1000 acre.

of the area of the other types. If these two adjustments could be made, the extent of the failure in these other types would probably amount to about one-quarter or more of the area cut over.

Moreover it should not be overlooked that even within areas where average stocking percentages are higher than the minimum of 20, there are portions, sometimes of considerable size, that are understocked. This is indicated by the low average stocking percentages obtained for spruce and the medium stocking percentages obtained for balsam on many sites (see Tables I and II). Personal observations on cut-over areas throughout the Province provide further evidence of understocking. The estimate that one-quarter of the area of the types, other than the swamps, should be classed as a failure is therefore believed to be a conservative one.

These considerations are all based on the assumption that when less than 20 per cent of the quadrats (of 1/1000 acre size) taken on an area are stocked to either spruce or balsam, the area should be classed as a failure. That may be too high a standard to set, although there is no evidence that such is the case.

For the Province as a whole, it may be said that probably not less than one-quarter and perhaps as much as one-third of the area that has been cut over and not burned and that occurs in the pulpwood types, other than the black spruce swamps, is at present too poorly stocked with spruce, or balsam, or jack pine to provide a profitable cut of conifers at the end of the present rotation. If the area of cut-over that has been burned is included, it is then probable that as much as one-half of the cut-over land on these types is insufficiently stocked.

On the remainder of the cut-over land in these types there should be, barring accident, a profitable cut of conifers, although it is doubtful whether any great portion of the area within these types will provide a cut greater than that which was harvested. The heavy stands that have been cut in these types had their origin following forest fires that destroyed previous uncut stands. Thus the areas on which they occurred had the advantages of good seedbeds, protection for the establishment of seedlings, and a minimum of competition—three features that do not characterize cut-over land except in part in the swamps.

There is general agreement throughout the reports reviewed that the regeneration on cut-over areas in the black spruce swamp type, except where very wet, is good. It is, then, on the better drained areas of high productive capacity that regeneration is the poorest, and it is the cut-over land on these sites that gives the least promise.

ANALYSIS OF PROCEDURE IN CARRYING OUT AND REPORTING REGENERATION SURVEYS

THE views of many persons concerned with the nature of forest regeneration on cut-over and burned forest land are based mainly on the surveys for which there are written reports. It is important therefore that precautions be taken to ensure accurate field recordings, and that these be correctly interpreted and presented in a readily understandable form. Otherwise the views obtained are liable to serious error.

Whether or not these requirements have been met or whether it has been possible to meet them is revealed through an examination of the procedure followed in carrying out the surveys and in reporting them.

The main purpose of this analysis is to determine any features of the regeneration surveys that tend to reduce their value in providing reliable information concerning the nature and extent of forest regeneration on disturbed forest land. For convenience the features are discussed under the headings, Field Work and Interpretation of Data, Reports, and Personnel.

FIELD WORK AND INTERPRETATION OF DATA

Until about 1040 the tally plot method of recording regeneration was used. Different sizes of plot were adopted, the commonest being one-twentieth of an acre in area. On each plot a stem count was made of the tree species being studied. An arbitrary diameter was fixed as the upper limit of reproduction and generally an attempt was made, usually on the basis of height, to separate reproduction since logging or other disturbances from advance growth. Plot tallies were converted to numbers per acre so that the results for one area could be compared with those obtained on others.

Owing to the large size of the plots it was rarely possible to examine enough of them within an area to get a representative sample. This was particularly unfortunate on areas where conditions were not uniform. On such areas the plots were not always typical of conditions and the number of stems per acre derived from them could be misleading. Thus two areas shown to have the same number of stems per acre could be very different from one another. In one case the stems might be distributed over the whole area while in the other they might be concentrated on certain portions only. The number of stems per acre thus failed to indicate their distribution.

The stocked quadrat was introduced about 1940 for the purpose of reducing the uncertainty of meaning of stocking figures based solely on the average number of seedlings per acre. It developed from the assumption that if an area is broken up into small squares of the size required for a mature tree and if on each of these there is found an established seedling of the species desired, the area may be said to be fully stocked. If however only a fraction of the squares have seedlings then the area is understocked. The degree of understocking is indicated by the size of the fraction obtained. Thus if half the squares have seedlings the stocking would be 50 per cent—the area is half stocked; 20 per cent stocking indicates that one-fifth of the area is stocked. The fact that some squares have several individuals is disregarded, it being assumed that only one will survive till maturity.

Since it would be impracticable to examine all the squares on any sizeable area a systematic sample only is made. The squares, or quadrats, are taken at intervals along a compass line run through the area being sampled. Each quadrat examined is recorded as stocked, or unstocked, to the species being considered. In this way it is possible to cover a considerable area and thus obtain a sample of the variations that naturally occur in any sizeable stand. Also, if on a small number of the quadrats a complete count of all the individuals of each species is made then the average number per acre can be determined for each species.

The method thus gives, in addition to the probable number of individuals occurring on an area, some idea of the manner of their distribution. It is generally considered to be the best known method of sampling the reproduction on extensive areas and although it does not fully satisfy all the requirements for accurate sampling it does make it possible to obtain an index of stocking that is probably as useful and reliable as present requirements demand and certainly more dependable than that provided by stocking figures based solely on the average number of trees per acre obtained from a relatively small number of large plots.

In the application of the stocked quadrat method, however, there are a few irregularities, due largely to differences of opinion regarding the reliability of the stocking indices obtained. Different sizes of quadrat are in use, the two commonest being one-thousandth and one-six-hundredth of an acre. In some cases the quadrats are taken singly and distributed fairly uniformly over the area investigated. In other cases they are taken in groups of from four to twenty, the groups being distributed over the area. The distance separating single quadrats or groups of quadrats, taken on a line, varies as well as the distance separating the lines. Different kinds of tally sheets are in use so that there are different ways of recording observations. Some tally sheets are designed to prevent errors in recording, others are not. One, the punch card, is designed for greater ease in the recording, compilation, and analysis of the data.

In addition there are a number of uncertainties confronting the field worker. Of particular importance are the problems relating to such matters as recognizing forest types, advance growth, reproduction since logging, layerings, and the use of stocking percentages.

There are then seven rather important factors that affect in varying degree the reliability of survey data and their interpretation. These are: quadrat size, quadrat distribution, tallying, forest types, kinds of regeneration, stocking percentages, and stocking standards.

1. *Quadrat Size*

The larger the size of quadrat used the greater the chance of reproduction being present. This influences the stocking percentages so that one cannot compare directly the results obtained in surveys where different sizes of quadrat have been used.

The natural tendency of the reader of reports is, of course, to accept the stocking percentages as given. If they are high for one type in a given report and low for a different type in another report, the former will usually be considered as better stocked. The fact that much of the apparent difference between the two types may be due to a difference in quadrat size is not apparent. It is true that the size of quadrat used in each case will be given but neither the reader nor the investigator may be aware of its significance.

The introduction of a method[9] of converting stocking percentages to equivalents based on a common size of quadrat may overcome much of this difficulty, although there still remains the problem of determining the size of quadrat that will give the most reliable meaning to stocking percentages.

At the present time, therefore, it would seem desirable to adopt a uniform size of quadrat, one that will satisfy the requirements for accuracy of recording and at the same time give to all stocking percentages obtained a comparable value. If at some future date it should be discovered that a different size would better express these values the figures could be converted to equivalents of that size. In the

[9]See above, note 3.

meantime one of the difficulties of comparing results obtained in different surveys would be eliminated.

The adoption of a small quadrat would also seem to be desirable, as this would reduce the opportunity for error in field recording. Large quadrats are more difficult to observe accurately than small ones: the field worker generally finds it necessary to divide the quadrat and examine each part separately with the danger that one or more may be overlooked. Also, the boundaries of the large quadrat are more apt to be wrongly located. These facts all suggest the desirability of using a small size of quadrat.

2. Quadrat Distribution

Two different ways of distributing quadrats over the area being surveyed are in common use. By some investigators the quadrats are grouped, 20 being taken in sequence along a line, with groups, or "plots," separated by intervals of four chains. Thus in a distance of three-quarters of a mile, 10 "plots," each comprising 20 quadrats, or a total of 200 quadrats, are examined. The majority of the investigators, however, take only one quadrat, usually at the end of each chain. Thus to examine 200 the investigator must cover two and one-half miles.

While both methods may give sufficiently reliable stocking percentages it is doubtful whether those obtained from grouped quadrats are as accurate as those from quadrats placed singly. Grouping reduces the opportunity of obtaining representative data since fewer different parts of the area are sampled.

One of the main reasons for adopting the quadrat system was to ensure the examination of many different parts of any area surveyed. By using small plots (quadrats) instead of large plots this would be possible, and provided the quadrats are well distributed there should be a good chance of including all the variations that occur. To group these quadrats reduces this possibility.

The adoption of the single quadrat method should remove some of the doubt as to the value of stocking percentages.

3. Tallying

The fact that regeneration surveys are often carried out under difficult and trying conditions makes it necessary, for accuracy of recording, that the tally card used be of the type designed to prevent errors. The tally sheets introduced about 1935 by the Spruce Falls Power and Paper Company meet this requirement to a greater degree than any others now in use. The punch card used by the Forestry

Branch has some advantages over all the other tally forms, particularly when the data of a survey are being compiled. It may be possible to combine the good features of these two in one tally sheet. A detailed account of these two methods of tallying with sample tally sheets will be found in the appendix following Part I of this review.

4. Kinds of Regeneration

In most surveys advance growth is separated from reproduction since logging and in some cases layerings are differentiated. For various reasons faulty recording of these different kinds of reproduction is common. Advance growth is often mistaken for reproduction since logging. Layerings are easier to recognize, although in certain situations, for instance where sphagnum moss is growing rapidly, they may be mistaken for seedlings. The possibility of mistaking seedlings since logging for advance growth is slight. Thus any errors that are made will almost certainly result in too large a proportion of the regeneration being classed as reproduction that has come in since the disturbance.

The recording of a portion of the layerings or of the advance growth as seedlings that have occurred since logging is responsible for the belief in some quarters that cut-over areas are still seeding in to spruce and that their spruce content will therefore improve with time. There are instances where this is undoubtedly true, but in many cases logging has left the seedbed in a condition that is not favourable to the seeding-in of any tree species.

The fact is that regeneration surveys do not permit accurate determination of these different types of reproduction. The practice should be discontinued and where it is necessary to distinguish them a separate study should be undertaken by a qualified investigator.

5. Forest Types

Because of the variable nature of the forest in which the sampling is done it is necessary to classify it by cover types or some other means. Each investigator has therefore to outline a scheme of classification for the use of his field workers and to train them in the recognition of types. No standard classification is available for this purpose. The difficulties are further increased because of past logging and fire. As a result the types similarly designated in different surveys are not always comparable, and it is sometimes impossible to be sure that the stocking percentages obtained by one investigator for a forest type are comparable with those obtained by another investigator for what is stated to be the same type. Moreover, failure to recognize differences in type results in the combining of data for two or more types and thus non-typical stocking percentages are obtained.

Without a standard classification of forest types covering the Province there is uncertainty not only regarding the stocking percentages obtained for different forest types, but perhaps also in the evaluation of the results of other forest research projects.

6. Stocking Percentages

It is rather common practice to use stocking percentages to indicate numbers of stems per acre. Thus, based on a quadrat size of 1/1000 acre, a stocking percentage of 50 is sometimes interpreted as meaning that there are at least 500 stems per acre; one of 20 would mean at least 200 per acre. In the recent report of the Forestry Branch (No. 10) the reader is advised to adopt this interpretation if objection is taken to the stocking percentages. Such an interpretation is misleading and almost completely obscures the main purpose of these percentages. They are essentially *indices of distribution*, not of average numbers per acre.

It may be correct sometimes to use high stocking percentages for an estimate of the number of stems per acre. These indicate uniformity of distribution and for the areas on which they were obtained their use to indicate also an average per acre is not unreasonable. Low percentages, however, indicate lack of uniformity and the realization of this is lost as soon as the percentages are converted to numbers per acre. A low stocking percentage of 20 interpreted as an average of at least 200 trees per acre gives the reader the impression that over the area as a whole there are 200 trees per acre. Such an interpretation may lead to the conclusion that the area is considerably better stocked than is actually the case. The reader loses sight of the fact that some parts of the area may be fully stocked, other parts only partly stocked, and that perhaps more than half of it, even three-quarters, may be without trees.

If stocking percentages were referred to as frequency of occurrence figures there would be less danger of their being used to indicate the actual stocking.

The misuse of stocking percentages and the incorrect reporting of reproduction since logging have probably contributed more than anything else to disagreement regarding the nature of forest regeneration on cut-over land.

7. Stocking Standards

The main purpose of a regeneration survey is to report the quantity and distribution of regeneration, so that from this report may be learned the extent to which cut-over and burned-over land is being reproduced to desirable species. Quantities are given in numbers per acre and distribution in stocking percentages, or frequency of occurrence figures.

It becomes necessary then to indicate in some way the values of the figures obtained. For this purpose stocking standards have been used by some investigators. Those used by the Forestry Branch are: fully stocked, 80–100 per cent; well stocked, 60–79; moderately stocked, 40 to 59; understocked, 20 to 39; and failure, under 20 per cent. These are applied to stocking percentages obtained through the use of a quadrat size of 1/1000 acre. The Great Lakes Paper Company, using a 1/600-acre quadrat, applies the following standards: fully stocked, 90 to 100 per cent; well-stocked spruce swamps, 50 to 89, uplands, 60 to 89; moderately stocked spruce swamps, 40 to 49, uplands, 40 to 59; poorly stocked, 20 to 39; and failure, below 20 per cent.

In both these cases any area with a stocking below 20 per cent is classed as a failure. But 20 per cent stocking obtained when using a quadrat size of 1/600 acre is equivalent to 13 per cent stocking obtained by the use of 1/1000-acre quadrats. Thus the standard of failure set by the Company is considerably lower than that set by the Forestry Branch.

The use of standards has the effect of suggesting future possibilities. Areas classed as failures are looked upon as being inadequately stocked to produce a merchantable crop. This suggestion raises the question, What is adequate stocking? Some will consider 20 per cent too high, others will consider it too low, to be the indication of adequacy and will point out that the significance of the 20 depends not only on the size of quadrat used but also on whether or not the area is still seeding-in, on the age of the cutover, on the species that are present on the area, and on many other factors.

Undoubtedly there are a great many factors involved which make it difficult for the interpreter of results to decide that any particular area should be classed as inadequately stocked. There is no difficulty with those areas that lack regeneration and show no signs of natural seeding, but in the case of areas with regeneration it may be claimed that since no one knows for any given species at any given age during the early development of the stand what stocking is necessary to ensure a future crop, any decision that is made is liable to serious error. For that reason most investigators avoid any reference to future possibilities and give simply the present condition. Thus the reader is left to decide for himself on the basis of the present condition and whatever other evidence is given in the report. That an incorrect conclusion is sometimes reached is owing largely to misleading information concerning the kinds of regeneration and to the wrong use commonly made of stocking percentages, that is, the use of them to indicate the number of stems per acre.

At the present time it is not known that any particular quadrat size will correctly express the real significance of stocking percentages nor does it seem likely that one can readily be determined. Thus there is no known standard of stocking for all age classes for even one forest type. To obtain one for the wide variety of conditions that exist would involve a great effort in forest research continued over a very long period of time. That such research would produce any worth-while standards is doubtful.

Tentative standards will still have to be set and doubt will remain regarding their reliability. Thus the training and experience of the investigator will continue to influence the opinions reached about his conclusions concerning areas that have been surveyed.

REPORTS

It has been pointed out that there are some important differences in the method of survey, some uncertainties in the recorded data, and certain difficulties regarding their interpretation. Naturally all of these factors affect in varying degree the value of the reports prepared on regeneration surveys. Here, however, the intention is to examine these reports mainly from the point of view of their value in presenting the survey results in a clear, readable, and understandable form. That they have done so in the majority of cases reflects credit on the persons engaged in forest regeneration studies, the more so because of the difficulties referred to above.

To give completeness to this analysis of procedure, however, it is necessary to draw attention to a number of faults that weaken some of the reports and in a few cases make complete understanding difficult or perhaps impossible for the reader. These faults include:

1. Statements that are not clear in their meaning.

2. Repetition of the same description in several places; for instance, when a forest type is described in several different places in the same report.

3. Ambiguous table headings.

4. Failure to establish clearly the method of survey used.

5. Careless presentation of data; for instance, the splitting up of stocking percentages into height and diameter classes in such a way that it may be impossible for the reader to calculate the number of

quadrats that are stocked with any one species or combination of species.

6. Appearance of figures in the body of the report which fail to agree with those given in the tables. (This may be due to faulty proof reading.)

7. Failure to include in the tables the number of quadrats on which percentages are based.

8. Excessive use of percentages in the discussion without regard to the bases from which they have been derived.

9. Conclusions that are not in agreement with the reported data.

10. Recommendations that are not possible of execution.

11. Treatment of estimates as though they were actual counts.

12. Failure to distinguish between conclusions that are based on observations and those based on recorded data.

Where such faults occur they are bound to have a discouraging effect on the reader and make difficult his true evaluation of the results of the survey reported. Thus they add to the difficulties confronting anyone striving to obtain a sound view regarding the nature of forest regeneration. Nevertheless, it is doubtful whether these faults have contributed to any great extent in the development of unsound views. Their main influence, perhaps, has been to reflect discredit on forest regeneration surveys and forest research in general.

PERSONNEL

It would be unfair to the research workers who have carried out regeneration surveys and done the basic and arduous work connected therewith to conclude this analysis without any reference to them. Theirs are the reports which have formed the basis for this review and which have made possible the attainment of a picture of the probable nature of forest regeneration on cut-over and burned-over land in the Province. That a few important details in certain features of their work and in the presentation of the results of it have been faulty is owing largely to circumstances beyond their control.

Of necessity a great deal of the work has been done by young graduates and undergraduates, the majority of whom had little or no previous experience. Many of them were just beginning to understand some of the difficulties of forest survey work when given the full responsibility of carrying out regeneration surveys and reporting them. One undergraduate completed two surveys and submitted two reports in one season. When one considers these handicaps and, further, the varied condition of the forest in which the work has been done, the nature of the work and the difficulties of carrying it out, and the lack both of training facilities and of agreement on many important matters affecting the surveys, it is impossible to have other than admiration for their great effort.

Notwithstanding these many difficulties they have made available a great volume of detailed information regarding the regeneration on cut-over and burned-over land and other information on many important aspects of the condition of the forest. Moreover, and perhaps in some measure because of these difficulties, they have developed within their numbers a splendid group of self-trained research workers which will prove invaluable in helping to solve many of the problems that will have to be solved if the forest is to continue to be of use to us.

FIGURE 2. Good white pine reproduction following conventional logging on the limits of the Gillies Brothers Lumber Company, Little Nipissing River, Algonquin Park. Logging occurred during a seed year. Young pine approximately 17 years old.

FIGURE 3. View in the same stand shown in Figure 2, where white pine reproduction did not occur. Conifer reproduction is mainly spruce advance growth.

FIGURE 4. Jack pine reproduction following logging, occurring only on the trails and other areas where the mineral soil has been exposed. View taken on a seven-year cutover in Algonquin Park south of Bissett.

FIGURE 5. View of young stand of jack pine and black spruce taken on the limits of the KVP Company, north of Ramsay. This stand originated following a fire that destroyed an uncut stand.

FIGURE 6. Balsam advance growth. View taken on the limits of the Ontario–Minnesota Pulp and Paper Company in the Cedar Lake vicinity. Previous stand was a mixed conifer–hardwood type (M). Balsam ranges in age up to 40 years. Two-year-old cut (mechanical logging).

FIGURE 7. View taken on the limits of the Great Lakes Paper Company in the Black Sturgeon Concession. A fifteen-year-old mixed conifer–hardwood cutover (M). Poplar and birch were not cut and sprouts of these two now form the main part of the new stand. Little opportunity here for seeding-in of any tree species. In places some good advance growth of spruce, as shown in the picture.

FIGURE 8. View of uncut black spruce swamp type (BSS) (merchantable), taken on the limits of the Abitibi Power and Paper Company, 50 miles north of Iroquois Falls.

FIGURE 9. View of black spruce flat type (BS), taken on the limits of the Longlac Pulp and Paper Company, near Longlac.

FIGURE 10. View of jack pine type (MS), taken on the limits of the Longlac Pulp and Paper Company, near Geraldton.

FIGURE 11. View of jack pine type (MS), taken on the limits of the Marathon Paper Mills of Canada, near Stevens. Small black spruce shown in the foreground are layerings from spruce that seeded in with the jack pine.

FIGURE 12. Close view of spruce slope (S) two years after cutting, on the Brompton Pulp and Paper Company limits, in the vicinity of Lake Nipigon. Spruce layerings, the only conifer reproduction, may be seen in the middle of the picture.

FIGURE 13. Patch skidding in mixedwood type (M). Spruce and balsam removed in 16-foot wood. Residual stand largely poplar and birch. Conifer reproduction mainly advance growth of balsam with scattered spruce. View taken one year after cutting, near Saganash Lake south of Kapuskasing, on the limits of the Spruce Falls Power and Paper Company.

FIGURE 14. Strip cutting in softwood type (S) on the limits of the Brompton Pulp and Paper Company, south of Lake Nipigon. View taken across strips two years after cutting. Very little conifer advance growth and little opportunity for tree seedlings that do get started to survive.

FIGURE 15. Strip cutting in softwood type (S) on the limits of the Abitibi Power and Paper Company, near Auden. View taken along strip road one year after cutting. A few poplar root suckers the only reproduction.

FIGURE 16. A close view of the slash in area shown in Figure 14.

FIGURE 17. View taken near Longlac of slash on mixedwood cutover one
year after cutting. Abundance of cones on the black spruce top ensures a good
seed supply. Seedbed conditions have not improved with the logging and where
they are good there is little protection for any seedlings that start.

FIGURE 18. Distant view of clear cut spruce slope (S), taken five years after cutting on the limits of the Longlac Pulp and Paper Company. Reproduction mainly black spruce layerings which are not visible in the photograph.

FIGURE 19. Close view of the seedbed in the same cut-over area shown in Figure 18. A loose, mulch-like, spongy, raw-humus layer up to one foot in thickness. A difficult situation for the survival of spruce or other tree seedlings.

Figure 20. View taken near Geraldton of jack pine and poplar reproduction on burned cutover four years after the burn. Previous stand was jack pine–spruce. The seedbed conditions have been improved as a result of the fire, but seed supply and seedling protection have not.

Figure 21. View taken near Schreiber of uncut mixedwood stand one year after a burn that killed all the trees. Seedbed conditions have been greatly improved and good protection for seedlings remains, but the source of seed has been destroyed.

CONCLUSIONS

THE uncertainties in survey procedure create many difficulties for the young and inexperienced investigators and have the effect of discouraging them and reducing the quality of their work. These uncertainties have been in large measure responsible for the failure of some of the investigators to present their findings in a readily understandable form, and also give opportunity for differences in the interpretation of recorded data, leading to confusion and disagreement regarding the nature of forest regeneration in different parts of the Province.

Until there is general agreement on such matters as size of quadrat, distribution of quadrats, method of tallying, definition of forest types, kinds of regeneration, stocking percentages, and stocking standards, there will continue to be doubt regarding the results obtained in forest regeneration surveys. The fact that some of these factors, for example forest types and stocking standards, are not given to precise definition, increases the difficulty of reaching a decision and emphasizes the need for trained and experienced research workers. Nevertheless, it should be possible to attain a degree of understanding that would at least raise the standard of recorded data to a point where much of the doubt that now exists might be eliminated.

It should not be overlooked that research agencies receive recognition mainly by demonstrating the value of the results of the investigations of their workers. The report is the medium by which these values become known. Any features, then, of the surveys that reduce the opportunity for the reports to demonstrate the real value of this kind of research work will impede its progress and the progress of all forest research and make more difficult its continuance. The importance of the report cannot be too strongly emphasized. Its preparation may be part of the work of the individual responsible for the field work but it is the agency employing him that must assume the final responsibility.

RECOMMENDATIONS

1. From the evidence in the reports that have been reviewed there appears to be a considerable area of our cut-over forest land, particularly the better quality sites, that is not reproducing satisfactorily either as to species or as to quantity. Furthermore, for many of our commercially valuable species little progress has been made in developing methods of logging that will ensure their adequate reproduction. While research will undoubtedly improve our knowledge in this regard, a long period of time will be required to obtain the basic information and adapt our operating methods accordingly. In the meantime the extent of our non-productive cut-over and burned-over land is increasing annually. If we are to stop this process and ensure the establishment of satisfactory forest growth on these areas, it will be necessary, in many cases, to resort to artificial measures—seeding or planting. In this connection it may be noted that even in those countries where the greatest advances have been made in the development of silvicultural systems of cutting, natural regeneration frequently has to be supplemented by seeding or planting to obtain satisfactory stocking within a reasonable time after cutting.

With these points in mind, it is recommended that the study of factors affecting the artificial regeneration of the commercially important forest tree species be intensified, in order that the method, time, and degree of seeding or planting required will become known and the costs of such work be determined.

2. Every tree species has its own site requirements and each its own characteristic features of reproduction, and these are largely responsible for the occurrence of the species in aggregates of more or less definite forest types. Thus the performance of any one species is to be recognized through intimate knowledge of three particulars: site requirements, characteristics of species, and occurrence. These matters are only just now beginning to be clarified for our important tree species. Their further elucidation will be an integral part of the research work required in solving the problems of both natural and artificial regeneration, and will also be necessary for success in any experimental cutting that may be undertaken. From this it will be apparent that the training of research workers should include a thorough grounding in Forest Ecology, better known in this country as Silvics, which embraces the mass of scientific information concerning

24

tree species and tree associations basic to Silviculture, the art of growing merchantable crops of forest trees.

Therefore it is recommended that a greater opportunity to obtain the necessary training in the fundamentals of silviculture be provided for the men engaged in this kind of forest research work.

3. Certain matters that are directly connected with the procedure in carrying out forest regeneration surveys require clarification. They include mainly the uncertainties regarding stocking standards, quadrat size and quadrat distribution, tallying, kinds of regeneration (advance growth, seedlings since disturbance, and layerings), and forest types.

It is recommended, therefore, that a conference, or series of conferences, be held where interested workers will have the opportunity to express their views and take part in the formulation of a standard procedure and terminology.

APPENDIX

Method of tallying used by the Spruce Falls Power and Paper Company

All quadrats are tallied on the stocking record sheets (Sample Sheet No. 1) and every tenth quadrat is tallied on the stand sheets (Sample Sheet No. 2).

On the stocking record sheets every quadrat is tallied under the sub-heading "quadrats," which is thus a record of the chainage covered. Any quadrats which are not to be included in the record (generally because of a patch of uncut timber or a partial snow cover) are also tallied under "culls." The quadrats for the record must be tallied once under each of the first four double columns of the tally sheet. Thus a quadrat must be either stocked or unstocked to spruce, and similarly for balsam, for spruce and balsam, and for spruce or balsam. If a quadrat is tallied as stocked to spruce (or balsam) it must also be tallied under one of the columns of the fifth (or sixth) division of the tally sheet. A quadrat is considered to be stocked to spruce if one living spruce, regardless of size, occurs on it.

The tally on the stocking record sheets may be checked as follows:

1. In each site the number of quadrats stocked plus the number unstocked, for each of the four divisions, must equal the total number of quadrats examined in that site. These same totals for all sites must equal the difference between the total number of "quadrats" and the number of "culls."

2. In each site the total number of quadrats with seedlings (seed.), advance growth (adv.), and seedlings and advance growth (S. & A.) of spruce must equal the number stocked with spruce, and likewise for balsam.

3. In each site the number of quadrats stocked with spruce plus the number stocked with balsam must equal the number stocked with both plus the number stocked with either species.

4. The number of quadrats stocked with spruce or balsam must not be lower than the number stocked with spruce or the number stocked with balsam.

On every tenth quadrat a complete count of the stand is made and tallied on the stand sheet (Sample Sheet No. 2) under various classes and sizes. The tenth quadrats are numbered consecutively, e.g. 4—I, 4—II, 4—III, using Arabic numerals for the line number and Roman numerals for the quadrat number. Old poplar, birch, and larch are recorded by diameters, and new growth by number only, but with an approximate average diameter indicated.

In the office the tally of each day or line is transferred to similar sheets as numerical values and the various checks are applied. At the conclusion of the survey the data from the stocking record sheets are summarized and converted to a percentage basis. The data from the stand sheets are summarized and converted to an acreage basis.

REGENERATION STUDY

STOCKING RECORD

DATE:
STRIP NO.:
LOCATION:

YEAR OF CUT:
QUADRATS:
CULLS:

SITE	STRIP ROAD	SPRUCE		BALSAM		SPRUCE & BALSAM		SPRUCE OR BALSAM		SPRUCE			BALSAM		
		ST.	UNST.	ST.	UNST.	ST.	UNST.	ST.	UNST.	SEED.	ADV.	S. & A.	SEED.	ADV.	S. & A.
1-P	STRIP														
1-P	ROAD														
I-M	STRIP														
I-M	ROAD														
11-A	STRIP														
11-A	ROAD														
11-B	STRIP														
11-B	ROAD														
11-C	STRIP														
11-C	ROAD														
11-D	STRIP														
11-D	ROAD														
111	STRIP														
111	ROAD														
TOTAL															

Sample Sheet No. 1

DATE:

LOCATION:

STAND _____ SHEET _____

YEAR OF CUT _____

PLOT NUMBER	SITE	ROAD STRIP		SEEDLINGS			LAYERINGS			ADVANCE GROWTH								POPLAR BIR.		LAR.
				0 - 6	6-12	12-18	0 - 6	6 - 12	12-18	0 - 1.5	1.5-4.5	4.5 UP	1"	2"	3"	4" 5" UP				
			SPR.																	
			BAL.																	
			SPR.																	
			BAL.																	
			SPR.																	
			BAL.																	
			SPR.																	
			BAL.																	
			SPR.																	
			BAL.																	
			SPR.																	
			BAL.																	
			SPR.																	
			BAL.																	
			SPR.																	
			BAL.																	
			SPR.																	
			BAL.																	
			SPR.																	
			BAL.																	
			SPR.																	
			BAL.																	
			SPR.																	
			BAL.																	

SAMPLE SHEET No. 2

Method of tallying used by the Forestry Branch of Canada

Special punch cards have been prepared (Sample No. 3) on which to record the data for each plot. On one side of the card space is provided for a record of regeneration, advance growth, residual trees, and stumps for each quadrat. On the other side of the card space is provided for the count of regeneration and advance growth on the twentieth quadrat. On the margin of the cards various factors are keyed and the appropriate value of each of these is to be punched.

The following instructions are given in the order in which the data should be recorded on the card.

(i) Plot Number

Each plot[1] must be given a number. No number may be repeated by any party during the season. When a party is divided into two crews, one will use even, the other odd numbers. When a survey begins on another area, numbering of the plots must continue from where it stopped in the survey just completed.

(ii) Tally by Quadrats

Two types of reproduction are recognized:

(*a*) Regeneration. This term is applied to tree species which have become established subsequent to disturbance by fire, cutting, etc.

(*b*) Advance growth. This term is applied to tree species established prior to the disturbance and which at that time occupied a space in the shrub layer of the original forest sub-type. (This term must not be confused with residual growth.[2])

The presence of regeneration is to be indicated on the card by recording the size class of the largest seedling (or sapling) of each species in the upper left-hand corner of the proper square. Likewise, the presence of advanced growth for each species is recorded by using the symbol for the size class in the upper right-hand corner of the proper square.

The following is a statement of the four size classes used to record regeneration and the four size classes used for advance growth:

Regeneration in Size Classes	Advance Growth Size Classes
1 = seedlings up to 3″ in height	A = under 1″ d.b.h.
2 = from 3″ to 3′ in height	B = 1″ d.b.h.
3 = from 3′ in height to ½″ d.b.h.	C = 2″ d.b.h.
4 = over ½″ d.b.h.	D = 3″ d.b.h. or over

The presence of a residual tree on a quadrat must be recorded by species in the left-hand corner of the lower square, the record to be marked by an X.

The presence of a stump on a quadrat must be recorded by species in the right-hand corner of the lower square, the record to be marked by an X.

The tally card has three horizontal columns headed "Stocked" and one vertical column headed "Totals." These are to be left blank.

[1]A sampling unit is a plot, and each plot is subdivided into 20 quadrats, each quadrat being 6.6 feet square.

[2]A residual tree is one whch formed part of the original stand but was not removed by the disturbance.

(iii) The 20th Quadrat

On the 20th quadrat a count, in addition to the above, is to be made of all regeneration and advance growth and this is to be recorded in the space provided according to size classes. The number of plants of a given size class and species will be recorded in the upper left-hand portion of the appropriate square, and the number of advance growth in the lower right-hand corner.

(iv) Data Recorded on Margin by Punching

After the record of reproduction for the twenty quadrats has been completed, the card is to be punched. In doing this, it is recommended that each item be dealt with in turn, commencing with "Party Number" and proceeding counter-clockwise, holding the edge of the card being punched towards the recorder. By following this plan, there is less likelihood that any factor will be overlooked and its value left unrecorded.

All factors punched on the cards will be related to the record for the 20th quadrat. That is to say, the density of underbrush, character of soil, crown canopy, slash conditions, etc. with respect to the 20th quadrat will be recorded. The factors, years since disturbance, nature of disturbance, and original forest sub-type apply both to the universe[3] and to the 20th quadrat.

Party Number. Punch the number allotted to the party. Example: for party number 6, punch 4 and 2 in the unit section. (As the party number is not changed during the season, this factor may be punched in advance.)

Universe Number. Each universe examined will be numbered consecutively commencing with number 1.

Strip Number. Strips will start with number 1 for each area. Where a party consists of two crews, one will use odd numbers only, and the other even numbers only. Example: for strip 13, punch 1 in the tens, and both 1 and 2 in the units.

Years since Disturbance. The number of years which have elapsed since disturbance of the universe must be determined. This factor is considered of major importance. Information may be obtained through records maintained by the Province or one of the logging companies. Failing recorded information of this nature, it will be necessary to determine the time of disturbance by counting the number of growth rings formed over blazes made at the time of disturbance on trees still living. It will be observed that in keying this factor time is grouped in five-year periods. It follows, therefore, that any determination by ring counts need not be any more precise than is necessary to fix such a period.

Nature of Disturbance. The factors considered are: Logging (L); Infestation (I); Fire (F); Logging and Fire (LF).

Original Forest Sub-type. This refers to the sub-type that existed before the disturbance, which may best be determined by an examination of the stumps. The residual stand may consist largely of hard-woods, but if the stumps show that conifers have been removed then it is fairly obvious that the original forest represented some mixedwood sub-type.

[3]A universe is an area, or portion of an area, on which one class of disturbance (logging, fire, logging and fire, insect infestation) took place during one five-year period and which was of one sub-type (original forest).

REPRODUCTION BY QUADRATS

PLOT NO. _____   DATE _____

SPECIES	1	2	3	4	5	6	7	8	9	10	11	12	13	14	15	16	17	18	19	20	TOTALS
Sw. Sr.																					
Sb.																					
Bf.																					
STOCKED																					
Pw.																					
Pr.																					
PJ PI																					
STOCKED																					
TH																					
IH																					
STOCKED																					

SAMPLE No. 3 (front)

FORM D.F.S. 801

INITIALS OF CREW MEMBERS _____

REMARKS (A) QUADRAT 20 _____

(B) PLOT

COUNT OF REPRODUCTION IN QUADRAT No. 20

SIZE CLASS		SPECIES						
REG.	A.G	S	BF.					
1	A							
2	B							
3	C							
4	D							

KIND OF SOIL						SOIL MOISTURE			DEPTH OF LITTER IN INCHES					
SAND	LOAM	SILT	CLAY	PEAT	HUMUS (ON ROCK)	DRY	MOIST	WET	3	2	1	½	¼	0

YEARS SINCE DISTURBANCE — 6/10, 11/15, 16/20, 21/+

1 2 4 7 1 2 1 2 4 7 1 2 4 7 1 2

UNITS | TENS | UNITS | T | UNITS | TENS

STRIP NUMBER | UNIVERSE NUMBER | PARTY NUMBER

NATURE OF DISTURBANCE: L, F, LF, I

ORIGINAL FOREST SUB-TYPE: SW./SR., SB., BF., PW/PR., PJ./PL., L, TH, IH

CROWN CANOPY IN %: 0/25, 25/50, 50/75, 75/+

DENSITY OF UNDERBRUSH: D, M, L, N

DENSITY OF HERBS: D, M, L, N

SLASH: D, M, L

QUADRATS REGENERATED: 0, 1/5, 6/10, 11/15, 16/20

HEALTH-REGEN. CON. HARD — H.C., H.U., H.H., H.U.

SEED SUPPLY (P / G): NIL, IH, TH, PJ Pl, PW PR, BF, SB, SW SR

SAMPLE No. 3 (reverse)

The sub-type will be indicated by punching out one hole to indicate a pure stand, or two or more holes to indicate a mixture of species. Only the principal species should be considered in defining the original sub-type and the species of minor importance should be ignored.

Crown Canopy in Percentage. Values are based on the percentage of shade provided by the residual trees. Example: if shade of the crown is less than 25 per cent, punch out the 0/25.

Density of Underbrush. The legends D, M, L, and N stand for Dense, Moderate, Light, and Nil respectively. Underbrush includes all woody growth such as hazel, labrador tea, alders, brambles, etc., and is quite distinct from tree species or herbaceous growth. Any species of underbrush which appears to hamper the establishment of tree seedlings should be noted under the heading "Remarks."

Density of Herbs. Herbs include herbaceous plants such as grasses, lilies, and all the annuals.

Slash. This is recorded as D, M, or L (Dense, Moderate, or Light).

Kind of Soil. This heading applies to the surface soil (upper six inches). If the soil is pure sand, loam, silt, or clay, punch the corresponding hole. If it is a mixture of two classes, for example clay–loam, punch the two holes concerned.

Soil Moisture. Punch for the normal or usual condition of the soil. This may not be the condition at the time of examination, as naturally all soils will be wet following heavy rain. The normal condition of moisture must be judged by the soil type, by its topographical position, and more particularly by the kind and character of the herbaceous growth.

Depth of Litter in Inches. Litter is to be interpreted as the layer of undecomposed organic material which consists of needles, leaves, and small twigs. For the purpose of this investigation, mosses and lichens will also be considered as litter. The hole to be punched is the one nearest to the actual value as determined. This means that the 3 will be punched for everything over or including that depth.

Seed Supply. Seed-bearing trees should be recorded if their distance from the 20th quadrat is not more than twice the height of the tree in question. Consideration must be given as to whether such seed trees are likely to provide a good or poor seed supply. If the prospect is considered good, the punch should be at G; if poor, at P under the species of seed trees present.

Health of Regeneration. This heading might also be interpreted as vigour of regeneration. If plants are in good health or vigour, the hole H should be punched out. If the plants appear unhealthy or of poor vigour, the hole U should be punched out. Provision is made for separate recording of the health of conifers and hardwoods.

Quadrats Regenerated. This space is for office use only and is not to be punched in the field.

Remarks (written). There are two classes of remarks: (A) those that refer to the 20th quadrat; (B) those that refer to the plot as a whole.

Both these classes of remarks are of major importance. The observer is requested to give as much information as possible under this heading, as it is felt that his observations may give several clues as to the reasons for success or failure of reproduction.

In commenting on the 20th quadrat, or the plot, the observer will deal with those factors which appear to him to have an influence on the abundance or scarcity of regeneration. Perhaps he is particularly impressed with the density of the underbrush or the depth of the litter, and although these factors have been keyed, nevertheless added emphasis will be given to their importance if they are again mentioned under the heading "Remarks." In some instances it may be observed that regeneration is limited to some particular medium such as rotted wood. That is a factor that has not been dealt with, and as it may be quite important reference should be made to it in the remarks.

General remarks should be made on each universe examined. These should be recorded in the space provided on the standard cards, using for this purpose as many cards as may be necessary. This is desirable in order that these remarks may be filed with the plot tally cards of the same area. The face of these cards should have written on them the words "General Remarks"; each card should be numbered consecutively, starting with 1, and this number should be followed by one in brackets to show the total number of cards used for these remarks, for example, 1 (7), indicating card one in a total of seven.

The party chief should make notes as the survey of each universe proceeds, so that, upon completion of the examination, these notes will serve as a guide in writing up the general remarks. Not to follow this practice is to trust too much to memory, with the probable result that comments will be weak and incomplete.

These general remarks should not only supply additional information but also provide the opportunity for making general observations, and for reviewing and highlighting the data revealed in the sample plots so as to depict properly the general over-all picture. Information should be given as to when the area was logged or burned. If logged, advise by whom, logging method employed, amount removed by species, general condition of residual stand (particularly whether it was made up of immature, overmature, healthy, or defective trees), and probable effect of this stand on the development of regeneration which may have become established. The remarks should also deal in general terms with the observed effects of underbrush, herbs, soil type, moisture relationships, depth of litter, etc., in the establishment and development of the regeneration. Where advance growth is present in appreciable quantities, its general condition should be commented upon and an opinion expressed as to its value in providing a future crop.

Part II

ABSTRACTS OF REPORTS, 1919–1951

FORESTRY BRANCH, CANADA

FOREST regeneration studies in Ontario, conducted by the Government of Canada, began under the direction of the Commission of Conservation in 1919. Two years later the forestry activities of the Commission were taken over by the Dominion Forest Service, now the Forestry Branch, Department of Resources and Development. Altogether ten reports have been issued. Four of these (Nos. 2, 3, 6, and 9 in this review) deal with three different field surveys conducted in the Goulais River watershed. One (No. 7) deals with regeneration problems on sample plots at the Petawawa Forest Experiment Station. Another one (No. 8) is a review of growth and regeneration surveys in Canada conducted by the Dominion Forest Service and the Commission of Conservation during the period 1918–36. The remaining four (Nos. 1, 4, 5, and 10) deal with field surveys in the Lake Abitibi District, Algonquin Park, the Sudbury region, and the Mississagi River and Cochrane areas, respectively.

In recording regeneration the large sample plot was used until about 1940. These plots were generally one square rod in area, located on cruise lines at varying distances apart. Because of their size only a few could be examined in any one survey. The regeneration was reported in numbers per acre. With the initiation of the Dominion-wide survey in 1945 the stocked quadrat method was adopted, and during the three years of field work required for the survey an attempt was made to develop a system of recording, compiling, and interpreting field data which would give a reliable picture of the nature of forest regeneration on an area. This aim was not attained, but certain features of the method of survey developed have been adopted by other agencies conducting surveys. An outline of the system of tallying developed has been included in the Appendix to Part I.

These reports, of which brief reviews are given in the following pages, constitute a large part of the record of work that has been done by different forest agencies in the effort to determine the quantity and kind of reproduction that follows logging or fire. They contain a great deal of information on these matters and on other important aspects of the problem of regenerating forest land. There is evidence in the latest report that the work now being done by the Forestry Branch in the study of this problem is directed largely towards the determination of the factors responsible for failure, or success, of reproduction on disturbed areas and the devising of practical means to prevent failure.

1. Lake Abitibi District, 1919: *C. R. Mills*

Purpose

To determine (1) the rate of growth and extent and character of the reproduction of balsam and spruce in the mature forest, and (2) the relationship between this growth and reproduction and that on the cut-over areas.

Area Studied

The vicinity of Low Bush, a station on the C.N.R. about 40 miles east of Cochrane in the Clay Belt.

The whole area was burned over, presumably 150 to 200 years before the survey. The forest at the time of the survey was uneven-aged conifers and hardwoods, the former predominating.

Method

Continuous strip system. Strips 1 chain wide and 20 chains apart. All balsam and spruce above ½" d.b.h. were recorded on the strips. At the end of every second chain a square-rod plot was marked off on which the seedling count was made. All trees below ½" in diameter were classed as seedlings.

Observations

1. Regeneration figures in numbers per acre show:

	Uncut area	Cut-over area
Balsam	3787	1280
Spruce	747	320

2. Many seedlings and young trees of both species are apparently killed during logging operations.

3. Still others are smothered out by the heavy growth of alder and maple brush and by the dense reproduction of poplar and birch which usually comes in on the cut-over areas, especially where the cut is severe and poplar and birch seed trees are present.

Conclusions

1. Spruce is being crowded out by balsam and is not reproducing itself sufficiently to hold its present percentage in the virgin stands.

2. In the cut-over areas, balsam is greatly in excess of spruce, there being plenty of balsam left but few spruce; barring accidents balsam will take possession of the areas.

3. If, when logging, all merchantable balsam were removed, fewer balsam seed trees would be left and the spruce would have a better chance to reproduce itself.

4. If, when logging, poplar and birch seed trees were removed, there would be less reproduction of these two species and the conifer seedlings would have better growing conditions.

5. Greater care to preserve the young growth during logging operations and a proper method of slash disposal would also have a good effect.

[Some of the conclusions reached by the author are not supported by the data given in the report. For example, there is no evidence that spruce is not reproducing itself sufficiently to hold its present percentage in the virgin stands, or that on the cut-over areas balsam will take possession. There is no reason to believe from the figures given that the removal of the merchantable balsam would give spruce a better chance. Several of the more recent reports by other investigators make much of the fact that there is very little reproduction following logging in the mixed type and that seed trees left on these areas are of doubtful value in adding to the quantity of regeneration. The removal of poplar and birch seed trees at the time of logging would increase rather than decrease the amount of reproduction of these two species.]

2. GOULAIS VALLEY, 1920: *McCarthy and Mills*

Purpose
To determine the influence of cutting on growth and regeneration of pulpwood species.

Areas Studied
Township 23, Range 11, and Township 24, Range 11, in the Goulais Valley, District of Algoma.
The area is underlain by Laurentian rock, with a medium to deep soil covering, except on the bare bluffs and hilltops which rise 500 feet above the valley levels. The soil is generally good.
Logging for pulpwood was carried out between 1905 and 1914.

Method
Continuous strip system combined with square-rod sample plots every 5th chain. Lines were laid out to cover 5 per cent of the area.

Observations and Conclusions
1. The present young growth was nearly all established before cutting.
2. Cutting has induced the spread of shrub growth.
3. After a fire aspen and paper birch take possession, with varying amounts of spruce and balsam following, depending upon the degree of humus remaining.
4. On very thin soils fire may destroy the soil cover to the extent that no tree regeneration will take place.

[This report, like the previous one, deals with a variety of subjects. Growth, utilization, and fire protection are the principle topics discussed. Regeneration occupies only a minor portion of the report.]

3. QUEBEC AND GOULAIS VALLEY, ONTARIO, 1923: *G. A. Mulloy*

Purpose
To determine the influence of cutting on growth and regeneration of

pulpwood species on cut-over land in Quebec and to compare the conditions there with those in the Goulais Valley, Ontario.

Area Studied

An area of 4,400 acres on Boule River (studied in 1918), Macaza River (1918) and Cache Creek (1919), all tributaries of the Rouge River, Quebec.

The report deals with the mixed type, composed mainly of yellow birch, red spruce, and balsam, which covers 59 per cent of the area and occupies the slopes and well-drained flats. The hardwood type on the ridges and the conifer type of the flats and swamps are omitted. Cuts of spruce and balsam, increasing in intensity, were made 30, 20, and 10 years before the survey, and again spread over the 5 years preceding the survey, although the Cache Creek area had only very light cutting in the decade before the survey.

Method

Strips 1 chain wide, and 20 chains apart. A square-rod plot was established every 2 chains for the purpose of analysing regeneration.

Types were mapped, including a division of mixedwood into hardwood–conifer and conifer–hardwood, but this distinction was disregarded in the report. Sites were defined as upper slope, lower slope, flat, and swamp, but no use was made of this classification in the report. An attempt was made to classify the stands examined on the bases of time and of severity of cut, but this proved rather unsatisfactory as it was not possible to determine the latter.

All conifers 1" d.b.h. and over on the strips were calipered and classified as free, suppressed, and dead standing. Hardwoods were not tallied, although apparently the hardwood main stand was tallied on the Cache River.

On seedling plots all coniferous small growth was pulled up, measured for height, and its age counted.

Stem analyses were made on the survey areas, chiefly Cache Creek, and on logging operations in the Upper Boule and Macaza valleys.

Results and Conclusions

Selective cutting carried on over a period of twenty-five years has favoured yellow birch and other hardwoods and the forest is now predominantly hardwood.

Spruce, which constituted approximately 55 per cent of the conifers before cutting, was reduced to 46 per cent of the merchantable stand at the time of survey, and 34 per cent of the trees were below merchantable size.

Figures for reproduction, taken from Table 35 in the report, show the number of seedlings per acre to be as follows:

District	Degree of Cut	Balsam	Spruce
Boule	Light (less than 10 trees per acre removed)	1053	106
	Moderate (10–30 trees removed)	1713	241
	Severe (more than 30 trees removed)	2477	422
Macaza	Light	1470	194
	Moderate	1284	244
	Severe	1543	530

The number of conifer seedlings seems sufficient for a new crop, but growth is very slow (Tables 31–4). It is pointed out that their distribution is irregular and that this lessens the significance of the apparent heavier reproduction on the more severe cuts. No correlation could be shown between reproduction and time since cutting.

In part, slow growth or failure of coniferous reproduction is due to the presence of residual hardwoods and dense raspberry and mountain maple patches. The establishment of coniferous reproduction before heavy cutting is suggested as a possible remedy.

The conditions of stocking and growth on the Quebec areas do not coincide with those in the Goulais Valley, Ontario. In the latter, the white birch admixture in the mixed type is not as unfavourable for the development of conifers as is the admixture of yellow birch that occurs in this type in Quebec.

[The number of spruce seedlings per acre given in the report for the cut-over mixed type in Quebec appears to be comparable with numbers found, not only on cut-over areas in somewhat similar types in the Goulais Valley, but also on cutover in the mixed type in other areas in Ontario; for example, Lake Abitibi District, 320; Algonquin Park, 100–580; Sudbury region, 1500–1600 (includes balsam); Goulais Valley, 76–222; the Clay Belt, 682. These figures are taken from reports of surveys conducted by the Forestry Branch. They have little value, however, without some means of indicating distribution.]

4. ALGONQUIN PARK, 1930: W. M. Robertson

Purpose
A rate of growth survey.

Area Studied
Sixteen representative blocks of 25 square miles each situated in the mixedwood belt of Ontario south of the French River, Lake Nipissing, and Mattawa River, and between the Ottawa River and Georgian Bay.

Much of the area had been cut over for pine and burned over several times, and was at the time of the survey occupied by second growth stands of intolerant hardwoods and white, red, and jack pines. Spruce and balsam were associate species. To the west of the area were stands of mature tolerant hardwoods.

Method
In each block a series of 50 2-square-chain sample plots provided the tree tally. Seedlings were counted and recorded by species on a 1-square-rod subplot on each plot.

The plot data were arranged under 9 cover types, namely:

> Jack pine
> Balsam and spruce
> Cedar and larch

Black spruce
Intolerant hardwood and pine
Intolerant hardwood and balsam and spruce
Tolerant hardwood and balsam and spruce
Intolerant hardwood
Tolerant hardwood

In the final analysis these 9 sub-types are grouped into softwood, mixed-wood, hardwood, and swamp. The results are given in Table IV, taken from Table 10 of the report.

TABLE IV

REPRODUCTION IN ALGONQUIN PARK IN NUMBERS PER ACRE

(BASED ON 800 ONE-SQUARE-ROD PLOTS)

| | Softwood type Age class | | Mixedwood type Age class | | | Hardwood type Age class | | Swamp Age class |
	0–20	61+	21–40	41–60	61+	1–20	61+	61+
W. spruce	14	49	107	160	44	26	8	26
Balsam	171	2831	767	2924	135	267	266	676
W. pine	18	7	82		23	30	8	3
R. pine	22		30	48		3		
J. pine	65							
Cedar		76	21	6	32	18	8	55
Hemlock		21		6	49		1	52
Tamarack	4							
W. birch	7	28	159	462	1030	580	152	2
Poplar	182		35	9	3	187	7	
Y. birch		56		17	36	5	148	2
H. maple	138	925	1531	1826	4596	2514	10,049	13
R. maple		257	259	248	116	472	33	
Beech			4	72	149	128	593	18
Oak	4		141	39	33	87		
Ash						4		
Basswood		63			201	4	49	
Hornbeam			4			1		
B. spruce			1					54
Total	625	4313	3141	5817	6447	4326	11,322	901

Conclusions

The author states that there is ample reproduction to take care of any openings that may occur in the stands but points out that balsam fir is the only coniferous species that reproduces readily in every age class, even in the hardwood and spruce swamp types.

5. SUDBURY REGION, 1930: *G. A. Mulloy*

Purpose

A rate of growth survey.

Area Studied

Approximately 8,000 square miles surrounding lakes Timagami and Wanapitei and along the Spanish River. All sample areas are south of the Height of Land.

Method

Blocks of 5 square miles were sampled by means of 100 mechanically selected plots of 1 square chain each. On each plot a tally of all trees 1″ d.b.h. and over was made. A seedling record was taken on a square-rod subplot.

Observations

In Table V (taken from Tables 13, 18, 23, 28, 33, 38, and 43 in the report) is given the number of seedlings per acre by species. Observations on the different sub-types were as follows:

1. *Balsam–Spruce sub-type.* Regeneration of the conifers is about the same in each age class (tree), varying from about 800 to 1500 per acre. It is therefore considered that there is ample coniferous regeneration.

2. *White birch–Aspen–Balsam–Spruce sub-type.* A uniform understory of 1500 to 1900 balsam and spruce seedlings and saplings per acre ensures that, provided fire is kept out, better stocking of the main stand will result and that, when the older stands are cut, regeneration is already started.

3. *White birch–Aspen sub-type.* It is doubtful whether the table correctly portrays the reproduction of white birch and aspen in this sub-type. The tally of conifers is probably correct and reveals from 300 to 640 per acre. These are mainly spruce and balsam.

4. *Jack pine sub-type.* The almost total absence of the intolerant hardwoods in the seedling stand taken with the rapid decrease in the representation of these species in the sapling stand shows that the conifers are regaining possession of the burned-over sites. The increase in the spruce and balsam fir seedlings with increased age shows the strong tendency of many of the stands now classed as pure jack pine to change to spruce and balsam fir stands.

5. *White birch–Aspen–Jack pine sub-type.* The most prominent feature is the large proportion of spruce and balsam fir to the almost total exclusion of jack pine. This sub-type is thus comparable with the pure jack pine sub-type.

6. *White pine–Red pine sub-type.* Balsam fir and spruce are the main species in the regeneration and the next rotation will see only a minor representation of white and red pine.

7. *White birch–Aspen–Pine sub-type.* Reproduction is largely spruce and balsam.

General Conclusion

With the exception that regeneration of white and red pine is almost negligible in most of the sub-types, the number of coniferous seedlings and saplings in the sub-types mainly represented would indicate that good regeneration is available to restock the forested areas in the Sudbury district. This is more particularly true of the sub-types where spruce and balsam fir form the coniferous component of the stands.

TABLE V. SEEDLING STAND

(Heights

	Balsam–Spruce			White birch–Aspen–Balsam–Spruce			White birch–Aspen				
	Age class			Age class			Age class				
	21–40	41–60	61–100	21–40	41–60	61–100	0–20	21–40	41–60	61–100	0–20
Spruce	22	194	185	228	129	132	220	91	179	70	369
Balsam	1180	1524	800	1290	1780	1530	200	202	420	344	
W. pine	22	14	51		12	35	42	4	19	25	3
R. pine	11										
J. pine							175	4			1210
Cedar		102	460		9	320	4		2	97	
Larch						3					
W. birch				66	1	3	550	170			
Poplar						1	340	12	375	3	20

[The survey on which this report is based was mainly a study of growth and was carried out, as were the previous Forestry Branch surveys, before the introduction of the stocked quadrat method of determining distribution of reproduction. Without figures for distribution it is difficult to evaluate the conclusions given.]

6. GOULAIS VALLEY (Research Note No. 36), 1931: *G. A. Mulloy*

This report deals with the 1927 resurvey of the Goulais River watershed surveyed by McCarthy and Mills in 1920. The data and conclusions are incorporated completely in Silvicultural Research Note No. 55, *Forest Development on the Goulais River Watershed 1910–1933*, by J. W. B. Sisam, considered as item Number 9 in this section of the review.

7. PETAWAWA FOREST EXPERIMENT STATION, 1935: *W. M. Robertson*

Purpose

To determine the relative value of (1) undisturbed litter; (2) mineral soil from which the litter has been burned; (3) mineral soil from which the litter has been removed, as media for the germination and development of conifers. A section of the report is devoted to a study of natural reproduction on abandoned farm land and the preparation of seedbeds.

Method

Sample plots, each 5 feet square, distributed over a poor variety of Trillium type (a dry sandy loam which once bore white pine and following fire produced a stand of poplar and an understory of conifers). The poplar was cut in 1920–1.

PER ACRE, SUDBURY REGION
up to 6 ft.)

Jack pine				White birch–Aspen–J. pine				White pine–Red pine			White birch–Aspen–Pine	
Age class				Age class				Age class			Age class	
21-40	41-60	61-100	101-140	0-20	21-40	41-60	61-100	41-60	61-100	101-140	41-60	61-100
134	193	340	308	580	207	291	214	425	199	167	260	225
28	397	184	298	35	78	199	380	173	226	1240	142	952
	26	24		7		11	16	10	134	254	55	28
								5		14	42	4
14	3	6	5	371	8	2		55				
					4	11	18	68		30	5	28
			5									
				140	26	5		5			5	
3				21	7	2		9				

Results

1. The number of seedlings found on nine subplots (total of 225 square feet) in four different years and the type of seedbed on which these were found were reported:

Treatment of seedbed	1922	1923	1924	1925
Humus undisturbed	23	27	34	28
Humus burnt off	193	100	112	113
Humus removed	853	1260	910	515

Average heights of these seedlings in the different seedbeds in 1932 were:

Humus undisturbed	0.6 feet
Humus burnt off	2.0 feet
Humus removed	1.0 feet

2. On the basis of results obtained from permanent sample plot number 41, Petawawa, the indication is that hardwood sprouts retard the reproduction of conifers.

3. On the basis of ten sample plots, numbers 44–7, 50 and 55–9, it would appear that complete regeneration of sprouts occurs within one year and that these do not persist to the detriment of conifer reproduction beyond ten or twelve years.

4. On the basis of five sample plots the following conclusions are reached with reference to reclamation of blank areas burned after logging operations:

(a) By exposing the mineral soil abundance of pine regeneration can be obtained on light, dry soils, except under very adverse conditions, provided suitable seed trees are in close proximity.

(b) Balsam fir seems to respond fairly well to the same treatment and on the same soils.

(c) It is apparent that these light, dry soils are not suitable for spruce.

(d) The survival of balsam fir and spruce that germinate seems to be satisfactory.

(e) White pine seedlings do not survive more than two or three years. 5. On the basis of two plots, numbers 60 and 61, direct seeding on abandoned fields or burnt-over land proved unsuccessful, but planting was partially successful. It is probable that one-half of planted stock will survive.

8. Review of Reports of Growth and Regeneration Surveys in Canada (1918–1936), 1938: R. H. Candy

Purpose

An analysis of the reports on growth and regeneration surveys conducted by the Dominion Forest Service and the Commission of Conservation in Canada up to 1936. (Only the reviews of reports of surveys made in Ontario and the references made to these in the summary and conclusions are referred to here.)

1. The *Regeneration Survey in Lake Abitibi District*, 1919, by C. R. Mills, receives the following comment: "The survey was conducted too soon after logging to furnish any definite results (the first cutting on the area was made in 1913–14, 5 or 6 years previous to the regeneration survey). The general impression given is that the whole area was badly in need of logging to encourage advance growth already established. In the mixedwood stand there is little suppression from hardwoods, so that no problem appears in this connection. A resurvey of the area would make the report of much greater value, as excellent data should be obtained as to what actually has happened on the cut-over area surveyed. Whatever reproduction followed cutting previous to 1919 should be a definite part of the stand at this date."

2. The following four reports are reviewed together: (a) *Forest Regeneration Survey, Goulais River*, 1920; McCarthy and Mills. (b) *Growth of Cut-over Pulpwood Forests in Ontario*, 1931; G. A. Mulloy. (c) *Forest Development on Cut-over Pulpwood Lands, Goulais River Watershed, Algoma*, 1936 (unpublished), J. W. B. Sisam. (d) *Forest Conditions Obtaining in Certain Cut-over Lands in Quebec and Ontario*, 1923; G. A. Mulloy. These receive the following comment:

"This study of growth on cut-over lands has been conducted in a most efficient manner in an area which is most suited for such a study. Sufficient re-examination of the original survey ((a) above) has been made to give definite indications as to the future position of pulpwood species following logging in these forests. It is noted that the stand as a whole is filling in with ample regeneration, but except for softwood types the regeneration tends to favour non-pulpwood species. Existing spruce and balsam fir are being suppressed by hardwoods in the mixedwood stand, particularly by tolerant hardwoods. The recommendation made in the report, that tolerant hardwoods be girdled, is strongly endorsed. The value of this interesting study would be greatly increased if plots were established on areas on which the hardwoods had been girdled. Girdling should however be restricted as far as possible to defective trees."

3. *Petawawa Forest Experiment Station*. A series of six experimental

cutting areas has been established at the station to study the effect of various silvicultural methods of logging upon growth of trees of the remaining stand, on advance growth, and upon the nature and amount of reproduction.

(These experiments were at the time of publication of the review too recently established to warrant any conclusive comment.)

4. *Growth Conditions of the Forests of Algonquin Park*, 1930, W. M. Robertson, receives the comment: "The rate of growth and reproduction seem very satisfactory. It is particularly noted, however, that there is a marked shortage of pine reproduction in all the age classes or types. It is possible that, because the stands are already well stocked, reproduction of this species is unable to survive. It is strongly recommended, however, that this problem be studied in this or a similar area in the near future. It is important to know if valuable species are likely to disappear gradually or return gradually, and to discover if any form of forest management or silviculture would be of assistance in bringing a greater proportion of pine into the forests in this area."

5. *Rate of Growth, Sudbury District*, 1930, G. A. Mulloy, is reported in part as follows: "The report states that spruce and balsam fir are associated with white birch and that the pines are associated with poplar. This deduction is confirmed by the Algonquin and Gatineau data. Further research should be made to determine whether the proportion of these two intolerant hardwoods, so common in stands of fire origin, can be used in site classification generally throughout eastern Canada. Excellent reproduction exists in this district, except for white and red pine, which is almost negligible in most sub-types. Spruce and balsam fir reproduction is very satisfactory and is taking the place of the pines. Even pure pine types have a large percentage of spruce and balsam fir in the understory or among the reproduction."

6. In the summary for the whole of Canada the following statements are made with reference to regeneration:

"Regeneration of pulpwood species is satisfactory in all the areas examined with one or two minor exceptions.

"The consistent success of regeneration on disturbed forest lands is rather surprising, but other points less satisfactory have been brought out in this general review. In the tolerant-hardwood belt, or in areas where merchantable conifers have been logged from a mixed stand of tolerant hardwoods and conifers, the growth of the conifers in the main stand and of conifers in the seedling and advance-growth classes is very slow. Although in most cases there is a moderate amount of coniferous reproduction in this type, its growth and development is so slow, owing to the suppression of tolerant hardwoods, that it seems most probable that if left to itself, the stand will remain, for all practical purposes, hardwood. [A footnote points out that information received from Lake Edward since the report was written tends to contradict this statement.]

"Another factor brought to light is the almost complete absence of reproduction of white pine, even in areas which are presumably its natural habitat.

"Speaking generally, information obtained from these surveys shows a promising future for growth, development, and regeneration of forest areas following logging, light fires, or insect attack. Though it is admittedly dangerous to draw final conclusions at this time regarding growth and regeneration on cut-over lands, yet a review of this wide range of surveys, and consideration of opinions expressed by experienced foresters give the impression that the problem of obtaining reproduction is not a serious one; in the majority of cases ample reproduction is obtained. It is possible to foresee that the final solution of this important problem will not be through the study of how to obtain reproduction, but how to manage the reproduction that already exists and the forests generally in order to ensure a satisfactory growth of young stands of desirable species in the proper proportions, and to see that a satisfactory proportion among species in the forest is encouraged. This is not, then, a problem of planting and seeding, but of better logging methods, thinning, pruning, and, to a limited extent, girdling, and possibly utilization of species now considered surplus and non-commercial. These opinions cannot be confirmed, but they should be entertained at this time.

"Surveys carried out in the province of Ontario have been made in widely separate types and districts—the spruce clay-belt of northern Ontario, the white pine belt of Algonquin Park and Sudbury district, the mixedwood belt of Algoma, and the well-drained pine and mixedwood belt of the Ottawa valley, represented by the Petawawa Forest Experiment Station. In all these districts the rate of growth seems satisfactory and the reproduction abundant. When the question of desirable species is considered, the situation does not seem so satisfactory. It is noted that the reproduction of white and red pine is very sparse, and the future of these species in their natural habitat does not seem very promising. There is every indication that, among conifers, spruce and balsam fir are replacing the pines."

7. In the Conclusions the following statements are made: "While these surveys indicate in a general way that regeneration in disturbed forests is most satisfactory, an analysis of the work undertaken indicates that such results should be treated with some caution at this stage of the investigation. Large areas or a large number of plots are compiled to show an average result without adequate consideration of factors such as site, vegetative zones, and degree and type of logging.

"Average figures for reproduction may possibly be misleading.

"Deductions drawn by the authors in some of the earlier reports on the condition of reproduction were in some cases not justified; for example, reproduction often contained a high percentage of balsam fir and a low percentage of spruce, and the author of the report assumed that this proportion of species in the regeneration would continue until they reached maturity. It is, of course, now known that balsam fir reproduction is not as persistent as spruce and therefore the latter species will probably constitute a more satisfactory percentage of the distribution in the final stand. In other cases, lack of regeneration in fully stocked stands was adversely compared with ample regeneration on cut-over areas or areas greatly opened up by budworm attack, and, as a result, false conclusions have been drawn; it is probable that the opening of virgin stands will result in sufficient regeneration.

"Considering the material that was available from these reports of surveys, however, the following conclusions can be drawn:—
[Conclusions (1) and (2) are concerned with growth and are therefore not included here.]
"(3) That with certain exceptions, dealt with in the general comments for each province, reproduction is abundant, and the reproduction of desirable species is satisfactory."

[The impression is given in this review that in general forest regeneration is satisfactory. It should be remembered, however, that the review was conducted too early to furnish reliable results. The author stated in his introduction "that the conclusions must be considered as being only of a tentative nature, and may require revision as more information becomes available." Today there is abundant evidence, in the many reports of surveys that have been made since the time of this review, that forest regeneration in general cannot be considered to be satisfactory.]

9. GOULAIS RIVER WATERSHED, 1939: *J. W. B. Sisam*

Purpose
The report is primarily concerned with growth and mortality following cutting operations, but also includes a study of the rate at which cut-over pulpwood lands are restocking.

Area Studied
An area of 41,000 acres near the junction of the main Goulais River and its east branch, in Townships 23 and 24, Range 11, Algoma District.

Method
Two methods of examination have been used: (1) by means of a large number of samples selected over the whole area in the nature of a cruise; (2) by means of carefully selected sample plots, each representing an average of a definite type and condition of the forest cover. Two cruises of the area had previously been made, one in 1920 and the second in 1927. Five permanent sample plots were established in 1928 and remeasured in 1933.
Reproduction (trees less 0.5" d.b.h.) was recorded on square-rod sample plots at 5-chain intervals during the cruise.
All seedlings were counted and measured for height on 5 randomly selected square-rod subplots per permanent sample plot.

Results
(Only those concerned with regeneration are summarized here.)
The number of seedlings per acre in 1920 and 1927, including those which had become saplings during the period, is shown in Table VI, taken from Table 8 in the report.
The significant points to be observed from this table are:
1. In the mixedwood type spruce seedlings have become greatly reduced in numbers. This may be traced to competition from underbrush, including hardwood reproduction.

TABLE VI

NUMBER OF SEEDLINGS PER ACRE, GOULAIS RIVER WATERSHED

	Mixedwood		Softwood	
	1920	1927	1920	1927
Spruce	222	76	179	303
Balsam	496	577	731	1041
Wh. pine	10	14	15	12
Cedar	663	758	590	1392
Wh. birch		12		8
Y. birch		18		3
Maple	1958	1461	123	186
TOTAL	3349	2916	1638	2945

2. In both types balsam is increasing, particularly in the softwood type. This is a further competitor of spruce.

3. There is a large representation of cedar in both types and a great increase in seedlings of this species, particularly in the softwood type. This is a serious competitor of pulpwood species.

In addition to these considerations it should be noted that a considerable number of the spruce and balsam seedlings were established before the cutting and are so suppressed that they will never recover and that the distribution of them is poor.

From 1928 to 1933, sample plot measurements (pp. 30–40 of the report) show:

1. In lightly cut mixedwood, spruce seedlings increased from 192 to 256 per acre, while balsam decreased from 480 to 352. Cedar dropped sharply while maple and birch showed great increases.

2. In heavily cut mixedwood, spruce increased from 0 to 160, balsam from 160 to 384, cedar was absent, and maple and birch increased less than on the light cut. In part this is owing to a lower hardwood content before cutting. Dense hazel brush interfered with early regeneration, but evidently conditions had improved in the period.

3. In the mature softwood cutover, spruce seed trees were lacking immediately after the cut, while mature balsam trees were abundant. Younger spruce were just starting to bear seed at the time of these surveys. In the period, spruce seedlings increased from 0 to 96 per acre, and balsam from 1088 to 1152. Hardwoods were negligible on both softwood plots.

4. In the younger softwood, spruce showed an increase from 448 to 544, and balsam a decrease from 2016 to 1600. Apparently in both softwood stands heavy balsam reproduction became established immediately after cutting, whereas spruce improved its position later, but rather slowly.

It is pointed out that in a comparison of the survey data with data obtained on the sample plots the actual numbers per acre given by the latter are of relatively little statistical significance; however the trends shown are useful in extending the earlier survey data to indicate the trend in the development of the stands from 1920 to 1933.

Conclusions

The cut-over areas of the softwood type are producing fairly well stocked stands of pulpwood species. On the cut-over mixedwood type, the pulpwood species are developing to some extent in the stand openings. The heavy overstory of non-pulpwood species and the underbrush produce a strongly competitive environment for spruce and balsam on this type. Thus conditions are relatively more favourable for the development of pulpwood species on the softwood type than on the mixedwood type.

Sufficient regeneration was established on the area, before cutting, to ensure a second crop of pulpwood, though much of it was badly suppressed. Conditions for its establishment have improved in the softwood type, but have become worse in the mixedwood type.

Girdling of overmature hardwoods and favouring of white spruce in the next cut are strongly recommended.

[Although this report is primarily concerned with growth and mortality following cutting operations the sections of it dealing with the rate at which cut-over areas are restocking to spruce and balsam (summarized above) give a very clear picture of the regeneration on two important pulpwood types, the softwood and mixedwood. The latter is the forest type that has been found, by many other investigators, to show the lowest quantity and the greatest irregularity in the distribution of spruce regeneration following cutting.]

10. REPRODUCTION ON CUT-OVER AND BURNED-OVER LAND IN CANADA, 1951: *R. H. Candy*

Purpose

The major purpose was to determine the extent to which cut-over and burned-over lands were reproducing in the various forest sections of Canada, particularly with respect to coniferous pulpwood species.

Secondary objectives were to develop a satisfactory system for the collection, compilation, and analysis of data from reproduction surveys, and to determine in general terms the more important factors in locations where reproduction following disturbance was unsatisfactory.

Method

The field data were taken on a plot consisting of 20 quadrats, each 6.6 feet square.

These quadrats were taken in one of two ways, the choice being left to the party chief: (*a*) A line of 20 quadrats, making a continuous plot 2 chains long and 6.6 feet wide; plots were separated along the line by a distance of 4 chains. (*b*) Quadrats in groups of four forming a square, the distance from centre to centre of each group being 1 chain.

For either type of plot the measurement between plots is made by pacing. For outlining the quadrats on the ground a rod 6.6 feet long is used.

All quadrats are tallied for stocking, the largest seedling and the largest specimen of advance growth for each species present on a quadrat being recorded; also, residual trees and stumps occurring on a quadrat are tallied on a stocking basis.

An actual count of the number of specimens of each species is recorded by size classes on each 20th quadrat. This was intended to provide for a comparison of numbers of reproduction with percentage of stocked quadrats.

For each plot (group of 20 quadrats) certain additional information is recorded, such as plot location, type, nature and age of disturbance, crown canopy in percentage, density of herbs, underbrush, slash, kind of soil, soil moisture, seed supply, condition of reproduction, etc.

For purposes of recording, the term "regeneration" is applied to tree species which have become established subsequent to disturbance. "Advance growth" is applied to tree species which had become established prior to disturbance, and which at that time occupied a space in the shrub layer of the original forest. "Residual tree" is one which formed part of the original stand.

The area being sampled is classed according to the original type, as softwood, mixedwood, or hardwood. The classification was to be determined from the companies' type maps of stands before disturbance and confirmed by examination of stumps and residual trees.

All field data are recorded on cards, 8 × 5 inches in size, designed for use with the punch card system, whereby cards can be sorted into groups for compilation by an instrument called the sorting needle, using the punched holes at the edge of the cards. For a complete description of the method of tallying see pages 29–34 above.

On each card, space is provided in the centre of one side for the record of reproduction on each of the 20 quadrats of a plot. Thus there is one card for each plot. Along the edges, space is provided for punching the plot data, such as years since disturbance, nature of disturbance, density of underbrush, soil, etc.

On the reverse side is space for the count on the 20th quadrat and for any remarks regarding the plot that cannot be punched.

In the compilation of the data from the cards, it is a simple matter to obtain for the area surveyed (or parts of it), the percentage of quadrats stocked to each species and the number of individuals of each species occurring on an acre.

In interpreting the stocking percentages the following standards were adopted for all species:

	Number of stocked quadrats per plot	Percentage
Fully stocked	16–20	80–100
Well stocked	12–16	60– 79
Moderately stocked	8–12	40– 59
Understocked	4– 8	20– 39
Failure	under 4	under 20

Results (Ontario only)

Two surveys were conducted, one in the Great Lakes–St. Lawrence

Region—the Mississagi River district, and the other in the Boreal Region—the Clay Belt district of Cochrane. The former was a centre of the white and red pine industry; the latter supports a large pulpwood industry.

On cut-over areas in the Mississagi River district the reproduction of conifers in the softwood and mixedwood types is "moderately stocked," the reproduction being mostly balsam fir. White and red pine reproduction is only 4 per cent stocked.

On the areas cut over and burned, coniferous reproduction in the softwood type is a 'failure' (13 per cent), and 'understocked' in the mixedwood type (21 per cent). Even the reproduction of white pine is a complete 'failure' (2 per cent).

On cut-over areas in the Clay Belt district of Cochrane the reproduction of conifers on both the softwood and mixedwood sub-types is 'well' to 'fully stocked.' (The sub-type is based on residual trees, advance growth, and regeneration. It might be the same as the original type, or might be of an entirely different character.) Black spruce is well represented in the coniferous reproduction in the softwood sub-type, but in the mixedwood sub-type balsam outnumbers spruce by 3 to 1.

On areas disturbed by logging and fire, the reproduction of conifers is 'moderately stocked' on both sub-types. Following this type of disturbance, spruce outnumbers balsam by about 4 to 1.

In the section "Discussion and Conclusions" in the report, the following observations are made with reference to Canada as a whole:

"In the general area from east of Lake Superior to the Atlantic coast, reproduction to conifers on areas disturbed by logging only is most encouraging. The reason for this is probably because the areas on which the surveys were made were, before cutting, mature or overmature. Such forests had long passed their maximum growth and, through mortality, were putting more into the soil than they were taking out. The stands were slowly opening up, and the ground was covered with rotten trees and decomposed or partly decomposed wood capable of retaining moisture like a sponge. This provided an ideal seedbed for coniferous reproduction, most of which was established before logging. Had some of the areas examined been logged a second time, or logged when the stand was much younger, and before advance growth was established, the whole picture might have been changed.

"West of Lake Superior, reproduction following any disturbance was much less abundant than in the east. This is probably owing to lack of moisture, in comparison with the east, and to a slower decomposition of the dry ground litter which has proven in many instances a handicap to the establishment of coniferous reproduction.

"In general, the survey showed that conditions of reproduction were quite different east and west of the Great Lakes, and much more satisfactory in the eastern section of Canada. It is important to keep in mind that across Canada, as a whole, the surveys were carried out on areas that had been logged only once, and that very severely, and that the results apply to conditions on forest areas which were mature or overmature. The results should be applied with considerable caution to younger forests which have been, or may be, cut over in future years."

[The author has indicated in his conclusions that there is some doubt regarding the value of the data recorded in the survey and that the results should be used with caution. Nevertheless it appears clear from an examination of the tables given in the report that for Ontario the regeneration of the desired species, such as the spruces, and the pines, is generally low compared with that of most other species. For white and red pine it is shown to be very poor.]

DEPARTMENT OF LANDS AND FORESTS

STUDIES designed to reveal the condition of the forest following disturbances such as logging or fire were started by the Ontario Forestry Branch in 1930 and during the succeeding three years seven surveys were made. From 1933 until 1945, during the period of reorganization and development of the present forest service, known as the Department of Lands and Forests, there was only one survey, in 1941. From 1946 to 1949 ten surveys were carried out and reported on.

In conducting these various surveys, different methods and techniques were tried and tested and gradual improvement in the method of recording data has resulted. The large plot size has been replaced by the 1/1000 acre size, and the list plot by the stocked quadrat. These and other changes make it difficult to compare directly the results of the earlier surveys with those of later years.

As a result of the large number of surveys that have been reported on by the Department, the forest conditions and the nature of forest regeneration in many parts of the Province have been pretty clearly revealed. In the recent regeneration studies the tendency evident is a departure from the practice of simply reporting conditions as they exist towards attempts to explain these conditions. Experiments in burning, scarifying, seeding, and cropping are replacing much of the previous regeneration survey work. These studies, however, have for the most part been of relatively short duration and have not yet been reported on. The reports that are here reviewed thus bring to a close the period of reporting mainly on the distribution and occurrence of forest regeneration.

The following six conclusions, based on the reports reviewed in this section, have been selected as the most important.

1. Jack pine regeneration seldom occurs on cut-over jack pine areas except where the mineral soil has been exposed.

2. Well-decayed wood, such as old logs on the ground, or well-rotted stumps, makes a good seedbed for trees. Species that are particularly selective, such as spruce and yellow birch, can on certain sites reproduce themselves only on such locations.

3. Following cutting, spruce regeneration has a higher survival rate than that of balsam.

4. The regeneration of tolerant species is mostly advance growth, i.e., it was established before the disturbance.

5. In general, logging slash is fairly well decomposed in ten years and has disappeared in twenty.

6. When logged, forest associations containing white spruce show no adequate increase in the regeneration of spruce.

For the convenience of the reader, abbreviations of species names, as used in the summaries of the reports of the Department of Lands and Forests, are listed below.

55

Symbol	Common name
Al	Alder
Ab	Ash, black
B	Balsam fir, Balsam
Bd	Basswood
Bw	Birch, white
By	Birch, yellow
Ce	Cedar, white
Ch	Cherry (general)
Ew	Elm, white
He	Hemlock, eastern
L	Larch or Tamarack
Mh	Maple, hard or sugar
Mm	Maple, mountain
Mr	Maple, red
O	Oak (general)
Or	Oak, red
P	Pine (general)
Pj	Pine, jack
Pr	Pine, red
Pw	Pine, white
Po	Poplar (general)
Pb	Poplar, balsam
A	Aspen, trembling
Alt	Aspen, large tooth
S	Spruce (general)
Sb	Spruce, black
Sw	Spruce, white

1. ONAPING LAKE, 1930

Purpose

To study the conditions of the forest following logging operations, with special reference to regeneration.

Area Studied

The Onaping Lake locality, about 50 miles north and west of the city of Sudbury, comprising the townships of Shelley, Onaping, Fairbairn, Scotia, Dunbar, Rhodes, Botha, Sweeney, Frechette, and parts of Emo, Dublin, Muldrew, and Beaumont. Only cut-over pulpwood lands unburned since logging were studied.

The area forms part of the Precambrian Shield, with rugged topography; it averages 1300 feet in altitude, and slopes gently southward. The soil is a glacial till, generally thin except in the depressions. Drainage is good with a low proportion of swamp.

Method

Line plot system with lines ¼ mile apart. Plots 48 feet × 45 feet comprising 1/20 acre, at 400-foot intervals. Data recorded included plot tallies, seedling ages, plot descriptions.

Observations and Conclusions

(Only those with reference to regeneration are included here.)

1. Regeneration type corresponds to cover type with the following modifications and exceptions:

(*a*) Jack pine is frequently represented in the cover type, but is not present as reproduction except under special conditions such as following a severe cut of jack pine where the mineral soil has been exposed.

(*b*) White pine reproduction is frequently found where the species is not represented in the cover type.

(*c*) The balsam/spruce ratio is always higher in the regeneration than in the corresponding cover type.

2. With the passing of time following a cut the proportion of spruce reproduction increases, owing to the dropping out of the other species.

3. Attempts to correlate density of underbrush with stocking were not too successful. It was apparent, however, that dense underbrush resulted in sparse regeneration.

4. Spruce seeds in very poorly after logging, but balsam continues to seed in prolificly.

The accompanying table (VII) provides a summary by associations of data compiled from descriptions of the cover types, and Tables 2, 4, and 7, given in the report.

2. Sand River Watershed, 1930; *W. D. Start*

Purpose

To study forest conditions, particularly the nature of regeneration on uncut lands.

Area Studied

Parts of Townships 28 and 29, Ranges 18, 19, and 20. The area is located about 75 miles north of Sault Ste Marie, west of the Algoma Central Railroad.

The topography varies from rolling in Range 20 to rugged in Range 18. Soil on the whole is good, the most common being the Parkin type (glacial debris of clay, sand, gravel, and boulders). Drainage is by the Sand River system and is excellent except in parts of Range 20, where black spruce swamps are common.

Method

Line plot system. Plots 100 feet × 33 feet usually taken every 6 chains (8 chains in Range 18). Lines 20 chains apart.

Observations and Conclusions

(Only those with reference to regeneration are included here.)

1. Examination of every balsam seedling on one ¼-acre plot showed almost 100 per cent infection with leaf rust (*Milesina Kriegeriana*).

TABLE VII

Summary of spruce and balsam regeneration by associations, Onaping Lake

Association	Period of cut	Age of stand	No. of plots	Spruce					Balsam			
				% layering*	% advance growth	% since logging†	Stems per acre‡	Ratio, regeneration %: cover type %	% advance growth	% since logging†	Stems per acre‡	Ratio, regeneration %: cover type %
Spruce–birch–white pine–balsam	1915	80–100	94	7	58	35	240	.29	6	94	1510	9.8
	1928	140–160	17	8	73	19	120	.34	37	63	1120	2.9
Spruce–jack pine *a* S 23%, Pj 11%	1915	80–100	21		81	19	100	.18	7	93	1520	4.2
	1925	100–120	13	19	56	25	70	.19	27	73	780	5.5
	1915		14	6	71	23	150	.30	8	92	1130	6.9
Spruce–jack pine *b* S 34%, Pj 20%	1925	80–100	41	6	66	28	200	.32	60	40	650	10.9
	1915		?	10	67	23	390	.57	1	99	630	9.1
	1925	100–120	27	15	60	25	90	.21	70	30	940	5.9
	1920		65	19	60	21	150	.40	56	44	900	6.4
Spruce–jack pine *c* S 37%, Pj 51%	1928	80–100	7	51	42	7	340	1.83	76	24	160	7.5
	1925		79	11	67	22	310	.60	63	37	300	6.8
	1915		52	12	72	16	510	1.02	8	92	570	13.9
	1925	100–120	71	11	62	27	340	.66	42	58	560	9.2
	1920		46	12	63	25	440	.77	53	47	730	10.4
Spruce–balsam–white birch	1915	140–160	9	31	50	19	70	.09	10	90	1680	2.5
	1910		50	11	58	31	150	.20	4	96	1690	2.7
	1928	160–180	39	21	63	16	250	.34	42	58	1270	3.0
Black spruce swamp	1925		22	14	51	35	900	.49	2	98	780	25.0
	1915		39	9	49	42	1020	.59	5	95	410	14.9
	1910		14	4	50	46	1390	.80	4	96	370	12.8
Black spruce upland	1920	140–160	12	23	45	32	400	.53	10	90	1800	?
	1915	80–100	14	12	55	33	700	.39	5	95	1640	13.6
Cedar swamp	1925		8		82	18	60		73	27	660	13.6

*Identification superficial, actual percentage probably much higher than figures show.
†Arbitrarily including 1-inch class to 5-inch class.
‡Healthy seedlings at least one year old up to 5-inch class.

2. Openings in the forest are essential for the establishment of white birch regeneration, and seemingly for that of yellow birch.

3. On one plot in the white spruce type, 61 per cent of the spruce seedlings were found to start in rotten wood. Yellow birch selects this seedbed also and balsam to a lesser degree.

4. Spruce regeneration, though sparser, appears to have a much higher survival rate than balsam, according to the tally on one ¼-acre plot:

	Total no. *per ¼ acre*	*No. of seedlings* *by height*			*Percent of seedlings* *by height*		
		1 ft.	2 ft.	3 ft.+	1 ft.	2 ft.	3 ft.+
Balsam	324	238	59	27	73	19	8
Spruce	39	16	8	15	41	21	38

5. Stems per acre of spruce and balsam seedlings on cutover number:

Association	No. of plots	Balsam	Spruce
Black spruce swamp	1	66	422
Spruce upland	20	488	191
White spruce	16	401	66
Softwood–tolerant hardwood	5	120	25
Tolerant hardwood–softwood	2	396	73

The accompanying table (VIII) provides a summary of the uncut areas by associations compiled from descriptions of the cover types, and Appendix B, given in the report.

3. NORTH BAY, 1930

Purpose

To study cut-over, unburned pine lands with a view to answering the following questions:

1. What are the relative amounts of reproduction since cutting and advance growth?

2. What will be the composition of the new crop, and does it differ from the old crop?

3. How much of the original stand has been removed, and how much is residual?

This survey is looked upon as the first step in the problem of working out cutting methods which will ensure an adequate regeneration of the most desirable species.

Area Studied

Parts of the townships of Lyman, Notman, Hammell, Gladman, Gooderham, Flett, and Hartle, lying between 12 and 40 miles north of North Bay.

The area is an uneven rocky plateau with a gentle slope toward the east and southeast. The underlying Precambrian rocks are frequently exposed, but otherwise covered to varying depths by glacial drift, forming a podsol type of soil.

TABLE VIII

SPRUCE AND BALSAM REGENERATION BY ASSOCIATIONS, SAND RIVER WATERSHED

Association	Composition	Site and soil	Ground cover	No. of plots	Seedlings per acre Balsam	Spruce
Black spruce swamp	Sb	Poorly drained low areas. Soil peaty	Deep moss; *Ledum*; scattered alder	59	170	286
Black spruce–cedar swamp	Sb, Ce	Poorly drained high areas	Cedar regeneration, similar to black spruce swamp	26	205	96
Spruce upland	Sb, B, Sw, Bw	(a) Well-drained moist areas (transitional) (b) Thin, fairly coarse sandy soils	(a) Alders and grasses or thick moss (if wet); or *Oxalis* and ferns with medium moss (if drier) (b) Thin moss, *Cornus*, *Oxalis*	263	366	142
White spruce	Sw, Bw, B, Ce, Pw	Low rolling areas, well drained, with a good covering of medium to fine soil	Dense covering of mountain maple, hazel, raspberry, mountain ash, juneberry. Also many herbs	610 *(19)	289 *(320)	52 *(67)
Jack pine–Spruce	Sb, Pj, Sw, B	Coarse sand, following fire	Thin moss with scattered *Aster*, *Epigaea*, *Linnaea*, balsam and spruce regeneration	2	130	101
Tolerant hardwood–softwood	By, Sw, B, Bw, Ce, Mh	Slopes of medium elevation. Parkin soil (glacial debris of clay, sand, gravel, and boulders)	Dense covering of mountain maple, hazel, and scattered mountain ash. Also ferns and *Oxalis*.	675 *(5)	140 *(149)	26 *(21)
Softwood–tolerant hardwood	B, Ce, Sb, hardwoods	(a) Steep slopes (b) Thin plateaus (c) Poorly drained spots in hardwood stands (d) Slopes of medium elevation in north	(a) *Lycopodium*, *Taxus*, cedar reproduction (b) Mountain maple, bracken, thin moss, *Cornus*, *Oxalis* (c) Red maple, cedar, mountain maple, and ferns (d) Mountain maple, hazel, *Oxalis*, ferns	139	246	30
Hardwood	Mh, By, Bw	Hilltops. Parkin soil of varying depth	Dense maple regeneration and hazel. Also *Rubus*, *Aralia*, *Streptopus*	469	61	9

*Indicates figures for immature stands.

Method

Line plot system with lines ¼ mile apart. Plots measured 46.6 feet square, comprising 1/20 acre, spaced 800 feet or 400 feet apart.

Observations and Conclusions

(Only those with reference to regeneration are included here.)

1. In almost every case, reproduction since cutting of white and red pine exceeds advance growth; it averages about 60 per cent of the total.

2. Pine regeneration is best on thin or coarse soils, presumably because competition is least there.

3. The best pine regeneration is found in associations where pine is most prominent in the cover type.

4. In all associations that have been cut the amount of pine in the regeneration is equal to or greater than the number of pine that occurred previous to cutting. There seems to be an increase in the amount of regeneration for at least ten years following a cut.

5. The regeneration of the tolerant coniferous species, especially balsam and cedar, is mostly advance growth.

6. Slash, particularly that of pine, is detrimental to regeneration because it kills advance growth and prevents seeding-in. A large part of the cut is occupied by such slash.

7. Skidding trails, skidways, and haul roads appear to be favourable situations for the establishment of pine.

[In this survey balsam regeneration is reported as being mostly advance growth. In the first survey made by the Department (No. 1) balsam is reported as seeding in prolifícly following logging.]

4. Gogama, 1931

Purpose

A study of the conditions of the forest after logging operations, with particular reference to the amount of advance growth present and the amount of seeding-in following logging.

Area Studied

1. The Minisinakwa Lake locality in the Central Divide about 90 miles northwest of the city of Sudbury, comprising the townships of St. Louis and Groves.

2. The Duke Lake locality, located immediately south of the Height of Land about 75 miles northwest of Sudbury, comprising the township of Edinburgh and parts of Arden and Vrooman.

Both localities are in the Precambrian Shield. In (1) the topography is rugged, the altitude about 1200 feet, and there is a moderate northward slope. In (2) the locality is largely an extensive sand and gravel plain, at an altitude of about 1250 feet, sloping gently northward to the Sand River. The soil is a glacial till of varying depth. Drainage is good except in the northwest part of Groves Township and the central part of Edinburgh Township.

Method

Similar to that used in the Onaping Lake survey (1930), that is 1/20-acre line plots.

Observations and Conclusions

(Only those with reference to regeneration are included here.)

1. Regeneration type corresponds to cover type with the following exceptions and modifications:

(a) Jack pine reproduction is insignificant in the regeneration, even where jack pine forms as much as 42 per cent of the parent stand.

(b) In the black spruce swamps and spruce uplands, reproduction of balsam and white birch forms a considerable part of the regeneration although these species are insignificant in the cover type.

(c) The percentage of spruce reproduction is always considerably lower than the percentage of that species in the cover type, those of balsam and white birch are much higher.

2. With the passing of time following a cut, the amount and percentage of spruce reproduction usually increases.

The amount of balsam reproduction decreases except where 50 per cent or more of the cover type is balsam, in which case there is a slight increase.

3. Spruce seeds in poorly after logging, but balsam prolificly.

[For the second time, in the reports made by the Department, balsam is reported as seeding in prolificly following logging.]

5. BATCHAWANA RIVER, 1931: *W. D. Start*

Purpose

To study forest conditions following cutting of pulpwood lands.

Area Studied

Parts of Townships 27 and 28, Range 14, and Township 28, Range 13. The area is located about 45 miles north of Sault Ste Marie on the Algoma Central Railroad. Cutting by the Abitibi Company for spruce and some balsam too place between 1914 and 1918.

The terrain is very rough with good drainage. In the valleys the soil is deep and loamy, on the hills thinner and variable.

Method

Line plot system, using plane table traverses of tote roads, or straight line staff compass traverses for control. Plots 45 feet × 48.4 feet, spaced 400 feet apart. A tally was taken of all trees on the plots. A description of each plot was made and notes of general interest were taken.

Observations and Conclusions

(Only those with reference to regeneration are included here.)

1. Balsam advance growth leads all other coniferous species in numbers per acre.

2. Spruce and balsam regeneration is best on moist or thin soils.

3. Advance growth of spruce and balsam is best in the black spruce semi-swamps and black spruce uplands.

4. Reproduction following cutting for all types averages 25 per cent of total regeneration; it is greatest on poor soils.

5. Layerings account for 5 per cent of the spruce and balsam regeneration. They are commonest in swampy areas and on black spruce uplands.

6. Reproduction shows a satisfactory increase in growth rate following cutting.

7. Logging slash was apparently roughly piled. After thirteen to seventeen years no reproduction has appeared through the piles, but as the piles do not cover any extensive area their adverse effect on regeneration is of no great significance.

The accompanying table (IX) provides a summary of the areas by associations compiled from descriptions of the cover types, and Tables 1 and 2 in Appendix E, given in the report.

6. ALGONQUIN PARK, 1931: *A. P. Leslie*

Purpose

A study of the condition of white pine regeneration on cut-over lands, unburned since logging:

1. To determine the conditions of the forest after the removal of the pine trees.

2. To obtain an estimate of the number of species such as pine and spruce coming back in the present stand.

3. To find the relationship between the number that came in before and after logging.

4. To study the factors influencing the establishment and survival of seedlings.

Area Studied

Parts of the townships of Bishop, Freswick, and Anglin in Algonquin Park.

The area is near the south-central tip of the Laurentian Shield. The Precambrian rocks are covered with a uniform blanket of sandy glacial deposit, with few rock outcrops. The topography is rolling, the mean elevation about 1100 feet, and the drainage generally good.

Method

Substantially the same as in the Onaping Lake survey, that is, 1/20-acre line plots. Examination was made of 1088 plots.

Observations and Conclusions

1. Under normal conditions, pine reproduction following cutting amounts to about twice the number of the pine stumps. It occurs in greatest numbers on the poorer sites.

2. Under normal conditions, reproduction that seeds in after logging exceeds the advance growth in quantity. It is composed largely of intolerant species. The advance growth is composed largely of tolerant species that were well established before cutting.

TABLE IX

SPRUCE AND BALSAM REGENERATION BY ASSOCIATIONS, BATCHAWANA RIVER

Association	Composition of cutover	Site and soil	Ground cover		No. of plots	Regeneration in numbers per acre				
			Before cutting	Effects of cutting		Total spruce and balsam	Layer-ings	Advance growth		Spruce and balsam since cutting
								Spruce	Balsam	
Black spruce swamp	Sb(57%), B(20%), Ce, L, Bw	Muck	Deep moss with scattered ericaceous plants and alders	Alders spread in openings	*71 8	1181	155	357	249	420
Mixed swamp	Sb(32%), Ce(31%), B(25%), Bw, L, Ab, Ew, Mr	Fine muck	Moss; or grass and herbs with alders	Cedar becomes dominant; alders spread	27 2	862	66	204	389	143
Black spruce semi-swamp	B(58%), Sb(15%), Sw, Bw, Ce	Wet soil or muck	Alders general and dense	Alders take nearly full possession	57 3	995	20	215	490	270
Spruce upland	B(45%), Sb(21%), Bw, Sw, Pw	Thin rocky, or sandy, or loamy soils	Advance regeneration, moss, ferns	Advance growth often stocks area fairly well. Soil dries and grasses increase	91 4	1052	32	228	585	207

*Upper figure indicates plots in cut area, lower in uncut.

TABLE IX (cont'd)

Association	Composition of cutover	Site and soil	Ground Cover — Before cutting	Ground Cover — Effects of cutting	No. of plots	Regeneration in numbers per acre — Total spruce and balsam	Layer-ings	Advance growth — Spruce	Advance growth — Balsam	Spruce and balsam since cutting
White spruce	B(42%), Sw(18%), Bw(16%), Ch, Mh	Well-drained flats and lower slopes	Mountain maple and hazel prevalent; *Oxalis*	Bronze birch borer kills about 10 birch per acre. Soil dries and hardens. *Oxalis* gives way to hazel, raspberry, and mountain maple	354 / 9	563		118	364	81
Softwood–tolerant hardwood	B(35%), Bw(15%), Mr, Ce, Mh, Sw, Sb, Pw	Steep rocky slopes			18 / 3	686	1	92	375	218
Tolerant hardwood–softwood	Mh(45%), B(21%), Ce, Bw, By, Sw, Mr	Upper slopes with medium to deep soils		Openings fill in with hazel, mountain maple and hardwood; soil dries	106 / 25	355		60	210	85
Hardwood	Mh(85%), B, By, Sw, Ew	Hilltops and higher uplands on glacial till	Maple advance growth		13 / 35	154		21	104	29

3. Regeneration on areas that have been selectively cut shows better survival than that on clear cut areas. It becomes established easily, possibly owing to the smaller openings in the stand, the smaller quantity of slash, and the presence of seed trees on selectively cut areas.

4. The largest numbers of pine seedlings are found on areas cut over during a pine seed year.

5. It is thought, judging from the areas where the largest number of seedlings occur, that if about ten mature pine trees per acre were left after cutting, the area would produce a second crop of pine.

6. Reproduction of all coniferous species appears to increase for at least ten years following logging.

7. The white pine weevil is active everywhere. Damage, however, is probably serious only in clear cut "pure pine" stands.

8. White pine blister rust was not observed.

9. Windfall damage is slight except in a few places where severe cutting occurred. Jack pine and aspen are most susceptible to wind damage.

10. Where cutting is at all heavy, slash is considerable and is a serious detriment to regeneration. In general, slash is fairly well decomposed at ten years and has disappeared at twenty years.

[The observation that reproduction of all coniferous species appears to increase for at least ten years following logging (6 above) indicates that in this survey it was considered that reproduction since logging accounts for a considerable portion of the regeneration found on cut-over areas.]

7. SUDBURY DISTRICT, 1933

Purpose

To compile a list, with descriptions, of forest associations in the Sudbury District, which could be used later in correlating the amounts and conditions of regeneration with forest associations.

Method

In 1930 and 1931 forest regeneration surveys were conducted in the District to study conditions on cut-over pulpwood lands. In 1932 a general reconnaissance was made to clarify these, and to extend the list of forest associations to uncut lands. In the regeneration surveys, the cover type was mapped continuously along the strip line and plots were placed at regular intervals. In the reconnaissance survey, notes were made on the areas in general and sample plots placed in locations considered typical. The report combines the results of the three surveys and attempts to classify the associations from a natural rather than a commercial standpoint.

Observations

The accompanying table (X) was compiled from the discussions of the different types in the report. Most of the associations are considered to have originated from fire with the following typical succession pattern:

(i) Recent burn—from establishment to formation of closed crown.

(ii) Second growth—until decimation of intolerant crown begins to open stand.

(iii) Transition stage—until decimation is complete.

(iv) Climax—when stand has attained relative stability.

When poplar, white birch and jack pine are not present in considerable amounts, stages (ii) and (iii) may be greatly shortened or omitted. Only associations in the last three stages are described. Tree cover only is indicated in describing these associations.

[The report is an attempt to classify the forest associations in the Sudbury District and its value in connection with forest regeneration is mainly to be found in the discussions on forest succession.]

8. The Status of Forest Research, 1933: *J. A. Brodie*

Purpose

To outline the progress made in forest research within the Department of Lands and Forests, in particular with reference to silviculture.

Observations

Forest research commenced in 1930 with studies of forest regeneration on cut-over pulpwood and pine lands unburned since logging. Three surveys were carried out that year in the areas of Onaping Lake, Sand River, and North Bay. In 1931 four were carried out in the areas of Gogama, Batchawana River, North Bay, and Algonquin Park.

A brief review of the reports on six of these seven areas is given as follows.

Onaping Lake locality, 1930 (No. 1, above)

Ten tracts of cut-over pulpwood land were examined comprising a total area of 24,000 acres; 848 sample plots were studied. Table XI (Table 1 of the report) gives figures for the regeneration observed on these plots.

Allowing for all known factors, spruce regeneration is adequate in associations 5, 6, and 7, while it is markedly deficient in 2, 3, and 4 and occupies an intermediate position in association 1.

Sand River locality, 1930 (No. 2, above)

The total area surveyed comprises 55,000 acres of uncut forest located in five townships; 2,200 plots were studied. Table XII (Table 3 of the report) gives figures for the regeneration observed on these plots.

Associations 1, 2, 3, and 4, occupying 41 per cent of the total area, are essentially pulpwood stands. Associations 6 and 7 are hardwood stands and occupy 22 per cent of the total area. Association 5, occupying 27 per cent of the total area, is mixed in character. In the two black spruce associations (1 and 2) there is a comparatively large amount of reproduction corresponding closely with the amount reported in the data for these associations in the Sudbury District. For the remaining associations prospects for a second crop after logging are not favourable since for these the next crop will be largely from reproduction that comes in after logging.

TABLE X

SUMMARY OF FOREST SUCCESSION, BY ASSOCIATIONS, SUDBURY DISTRICT

No.	Name	Main species	Minor species	Understory	Site	Age class	History and succession	Remarks
1	Poplar-white birch (PB)	A, Bw(80%+) ↑ A, Alt	Pj, Pr, Pw, Sb, Sw, B	Sw, Sb, B, Pr, Pw	Various, except thin rocky soils	20–120 E	F→1→7	Alternes: 3; P0, Bw; 2
2	Poplar-white birch-coniferous (PBC) (a) PB-spruce-balsam (b) PB-white pine-red pine (c) PB-jack pine	Po, Bw	Ce(20%+) Sb, Sw, B, Pj Sw, Pw, Pr, Mr, B Pj		Same as 1	20–120 E	F→2→8 ↗7 ↘9	Alternes: Po; Bw; 5; 3
3	Jack pine	Pj(80%+)	Po, Bw, Sb	Sb	Clay Belt: coarse or shallow soils. South: sandy or thin rocky soils	20–120 E	F→3→5	
4	Jack pine-poplar	Pj(80%−)	Po, Bw, Sb					F→4→5	Intermediate between 1 and 3. Alternes: 3; Po; Bw
5	Spruce-jack pine	Pj, Sb, Sw, B, Bw	Pw, A	(a) B, Sb, Bw (b) Sb	Various	130 150 160 E→S	4→5→(a)→7 ↘(b)→13	Chiefly in Central Divide
6	Spruce-poplar	Po, Sw, Sb, B, Bw		B, Ce, Bw	Various, chiefly finer soils	100–135 S	F→Po→6→7	Chiefly in Clay Belt as alternes in 7
7	Spruce-balsam-white birch	B, Bw, Sb, Sw	Pj, Po(10%+), Ce, Pb, Pw ↑ Pw		Clay Belt: deep clay Central Divide and south: Parkin and rocky soils	150+ S	1, 2(part), 5(a), 6, 8, 11 → 7	Alternes: 6, 8

† An upright arrow separates species found largely in the north from those found largely in the south. Other arrows (→) indicate successional trend.
E—Even-aged stand; S—Selection forest; F—Fire; Alterne—The term used for a variation in the association which occurs over a very small area (chiefly as an ...

TABLE X (*cont'd*)

SUMMARY OF FOREST SUCCESSION, BY ASSOCIATIONS, SUDBURY DISTRICT

No.	Name	Main species	Minor species	Understory	Site	Age class	History and succession	Remarks
8	White pine–spruce	Pw(25%+), Bw, Sw, Sb	Pr, Ce, Mr, B, Po, Pj	B, Bw, Ce, S, Mr, Po	Glacial till soils. Thin-soiled ridges. Coarse stony soils	90E 150S	1→8→7	
9	White pine–white birch	Pw(50%+), Bw	Pr, Po, Sw, Sb, Ce, B	B, Bw, Pw, Ce, Mr	Various, best in Parkin soils	150+ E→S	1→9→?	Found in small unburned patches
10	Red pine	Pr(80%+)	Pw, Bw	Bw, B, Sb, Ce (fi→Po, Pj)	Thin soils— rock, gravel, sand	→200 S	Climax?	Often evidence of repeated fires
11	Red pine–white pine	Pw, Pr(90%+)	Bw, B, Ce, Sw, Sb, Po, Pj	Sparse: B, Bw, Pw, Pr, Sb, Sw, Mr, A, Ce	Same as 10. Also with clay mixture	60–350 E or 2E	F→11→7?	Found near Sudbury and slightly north
12	Yellowbirch–hard maple–white pine	By, Mh, Pw	He	B, Bw, Sw, Mr	High plateaus or ridges: (a) deep, well-drained medium sand (b) sand-clay-boulder mixture	S		Largely destroyed by logging, fires, and clearing
13	Black spruce upland	Sb(90%+)	(a) Bw, B, Sw, Pw (b) Pj			75–150 E(→S)	5(b)→13	Widespread but infrequent
14	Black spruce swamp types (a) (b) (c)	Sb(90%+), Sb, Ce, B, Bw, Sb, B, Sw, Bw			Peat and muck soils	→250 S	Muskeg (a)→(b)→ (c)→7	Widespread and common

TABLE XI

REGENERATION IN NUMBERS PER ACRE, ONAPING LAKE LOCALITY

(848 sample plots)

Assoc.	Spruce			Balsam			Yrs. since cut	% of area
	Seedlings	Adv. growth	Stps.	Seedlings	Adv. growth	Stps.		
1	137	87	50	1130	427	0.4	15	15.7
2	73	53	30	1433	294	4.4	20	11.1
3	51	52	40	1025	542		15	6.5
4	76	64	61	628	297		10	11.6
5	225	68	133	438	141	0.8	5	23.8
6	610	317	188	362	93		15	3.7
7	253	273	101	1473	206		15	1.8
Miscellaneous								25.8

1. Spruce–birch–white pine–balsam association.
2. Spruce–balsam–white birch association.
3. Spruce–jack pine (a) (Jack pine 10 per cent and less).
4. Spruce–jack pine (b) (Jack pine 20 per cent, spruce 30 per cent).
5. Spruce–jack pine (c) (Jack pine 50 per cent, spruce 40 per cent).
6. Spruce swamp association.
7. Spruce upland association.

Seedlings—includes all reproduction under 1 inch d.b.h.
Advance growth—includes all reproduction 1 to 5 inches d.b.h.
Stps. (stumps)—indicates the number of trees cut in logging.

TABLE XII

REGENERATION IN NUMBERS PER ACRE, SAND RIVER LOCALITY

(2200 sample plots)

Assoc.	Spruce		Balsam		% of area
	Seedlings	Adv. growth	Seedlings	Adv. growth	
1	292	376	172	80	3
2	144	125	367	170	10
3	95	176	204	48	1
4	53	39	294	100	27
5	31	44	248	110	27
6	27	21	149	50	3
7	10	8	61	12	19
Miscellaneous					10

1. Black spruce swamp association.
2. Black spruce upland association.
3. Black spruce–cedar swamp association.
4. White spruce association.
5. Softwood–tolerant hardwood association.
6. Tolerant hardwood–softwood association.
7. Hardwood association.

North Bay District, 1930 (No. 3, above)

Seven tracts comprising 13,000 acres of cut-over pulpwood land were examined in seven townships; 627 plots were studied. Table XIII (Tables 5 and 6 of the report) gives figures for the regeneration observed on these plots.

A marked feature of most of the white pine areas examined is the small amount of advance growth that survives logging. The next crop will be produced almost entirely from reproduction that comes in after logging. Seed supply following logging is therefore a very important factor in the regeneration of stands in these pine areas. In the white pine association there are about 270 pine seedlings per acre. The remaining associations have only a small number of pine seedlings. In this district, maple and yellow birch, as they are near the northern limit of their distribution, do not compete vigorously with the conifers and stands of pine with spruce and of pure pine are common.

TABLE XIII

REGENERATION IN NUMBERS PER ACRE, NORTH BAY DISTRICT
(627 plots)

Assoc.	Bal.	Y. bir.	H. maple	Hem.	W. spr.	B. spr.	W. pine
			Seedlings				
By–H	718	81	329	17	20	42	56
M–By	686	133	1913	9	27	6	31
Pw–Bw	1142	11	24		23	68	95
Pw	1013	15	40		123	61	270
			Advance Growth				
By–H	117	20	16	2	3	6	0
M–By	141	24	101	1	6	3	1
Pw–Bw	224	4	6		14		2
Pw	199	3	1		19	20	4

By–H: Yellow birch–hemlock association.
M–By: Maple–yellow birch association.
Pw–Bw: White pine–white birch association.
Pw: White pine association.

Gogama locality, 1931 (No. 4, above)

Five tracts of cutover were surveyed, comprising 12,000 acres, on which 1300 plots were examined. Table XIV (Table 2 of the report) gives figures for the regeneration observed on these plots.

Compared with the Onaping Lake locality the Gogama area is marked by a larger proportion of the spruce–balsam–white birch association which here occupies over one-third of the total area. The spruce–jack pine (*a*) and (*b*) associations of the Onaping Lake area are absent but three additional associations are present. Of the remaining associations, the spruce–jack pine (*c*),[1] black spruce swamp, and black spruce upland are common to both localities. For the Gogama locality regeneration is relatively high on 26 per cent of the area surveyed and quite low on 46 per cent. It should be noted that the

[1]See footnote to Table XIV.

TABLE XIV

REGENERATION IN NUMBERS PER ACRE, GOGAMA LOCALITY

(1300 plots)

	Spruce			Balsam			Yrs. since cut	% of area
Assoc.	Seedlings	Adv. growth	Stps.	Seedlings	Adv. growth	Stps.		
1	120	18	45	2389	206	7	10	3.2
2	101	32	33	1895	215	53	10	35.5
3	675	212	292	145	28	1	10	4.2
4	263	75	41	2847	279	11	10	7.0
5	701	157	101	337	53		10	6.2
6	781	255	218	242	39		10	8.5
7	674	101	341	411	69		10	1.3
8	461	115	96	2060	185	19	10	5.4
Miscellaneous								28.7

1. Spruce–cedar–balsam–birch association.
2. Spruce–balsam–white birch association.
3. Spruce–jack pine–upland association.
4. Spruce–jack pine–balsam–white birch association.
5. Spruce–jack pine (c) association (Jack pine 50 per cent, spruce 40 per cent).
6. Black spruce swamp association.
7. Black spruce upland association.
8. Spruce–balsam–birch swamp association.

regeneration is somewhat better in this locality, particularly for spruce, and that the increase over that in the Onaping Lake locality is general and not confined to any particular association.

These two surveys appear to indicate (1) that the amount of regeneration both before and after logging is closely related to the composition of the association; (2) that the occurrence of the different associations and the percentage of the area occupied by each varies widely from locality to locality; (3) that the amount of regeneration in a given association may vary considerably in the different localities; (4) that an association with a high amount of regeneration in one locality will probably show a proportionately high amount of regeneration throughout its range.

Batchawana River locality, 1931 (No. 5, above)

This survey covered an area of 14,000 acres of cutover, on which 830 sample plots were examined. Table XV (Table 4 of the report) gives figures for the regeneration observed in these plots.

Here again adequate regeneration is found only in the two black spruce associations. Comparing these associations with the same ones in the unlogged Sand River area we find that there has been a fair increase in the amount of reproduction since this area was logged. Special attention should be given the white spruce association as it shows no adequate increase in the reproduction that has occurred since logging and has no apparent chance of re-establishing itself. Associations 5 and 6, both of which have a high tolerant hardwood content—maple and yellow birch—maintain their spruce content well after logging and it is probable that, through treatment, the spruce content of these associations could be increased. The hardwoods are of little commercial value, except for fuelwood, and since these associ-

TABLE XV

REGENERATION IN NUMBERS PER ACRE, BATCHAWANA RIVER LOCALITY
(830 plots)

Assoc.	Spruce			Balsam			Yrs. since cut	% of area
	Seedlings	Adv. growth	Stps.	Seedlings	Adv. growth	Stps.		
1	458	181	119	325	62	6	15	12.0
2	167	108	91	568	179	13	15	6.7
3	169	72	80	547	124	18	15	7.0
7	87	46	38	320	110	4	15	32.1
5	95	24	36	462	111	8	15	2.1
6	69	12	33	228	46		15	16.2
7	24	6	18	102	21	4	15	17.0
Miscellaneous								8.9

1. Black spruce swamp association.
2. Black spruce upland association.
3. Black spruce–cedar swamp association.
4. White spruce association.
5. Softwood–tolerant hardwood association.
6. Tolerant hardwood–softwood association.
7. Hardwood association.

ations occupy about one-fifth of the area an increase in their spruce content would improve the economic status of this locality.

Algonquin Park area, 1931 (No. 6, above)

This survey was carried out over an area of 19,000 acres, comprising six tracts on which 1100 plots were examined. Examination was confined to cut-over areas unburned since logging, although some parts examined had been lightly burned before logging. Table XVI (Tables 7 and 8 of the report) gives figures for the regeneration observed on these plots.

In the region in which these studies were made there is a tendency for all stands to revert to hardwood types. This is well shown in the tables. Even in the white pine stands, hardwood species appear to be replacing the conifers as a result of logging provided fires have not occurred. Both black and white spruce continue to maintain their position as a minor component of the stands after logging. Maple and yellow birch, although minor components in the advance growth, are the most numerous species in the seedling class.

A somewhat different picture is revealed by the studies in stands which have been run through by light fires and moderately thinned out before logging had taken place. This difference is well brought out by Table XVII (Tables 9 and 10 in the report).

Although many other factors may be involved in the variation in the regeneration besides the burn before logging, the interesting feature is that there is a much more satisfactory condition in the burned areas with respect to pine regeneration. The majority of the pine seedlings have become established since the area was logged and the marked deficiency of all species in the advance growth class is worthy of note. "The evidence seems to be quite consistent, we cannot log clear in white pine stands and get regeneration unless some accident such as fire has set up suitable conditions. Forest fires have accidentally in some instances set up conditions which have

TABLE XVI

REGENERATION IN NUMBERS PER ACRE, ALGONQUIN PARK AREA
UNBURNED STANDS
(1100 plots)

Assoc.	Bal.	Y. bir.	H. maple	Hem.	W. spr.	B. spr.	W. pine
			Seedlings				
By–H	2896	2907	9872	81	49	61	10
M–By	257	1154	49,920	4	10	1	7
Pw–Bw	3529	343	321	14	86	62	28
By–B–S	2157	6700	325	2	136	75	10
Pw	1696	340	1372	12	37	46	30
			Advance Growth				
By–H	205	15	17	18	8	7	3
M–By	97	12	78	3	3		1
Pw–Bw	624	8	6	22	25	29	5
By–B–S	172	18	3	1	38	8	1
Pw	468	23	11		9	29	47

By–H: Yellow birch–hemlock association.
M–By: Maple–yellow birch association.
Pw–Bw: White pine–white birch association.
By–B–S: Yellow birch–balsam–spruce association.
Pw: White pine association.

given pine regeneration, but that fires do not always have this effect is readily demonstrated,—other factors are involved." It seems probable that seed supply is a very important factor in pine regeneration, that the conditions set up in the soil layers by pine stands constitute another and that the vigorous competition of the tolerant hardwoods, general in all associ-

TABLE XVII

REGENERATION IN NUMBERS PER ACRE, ALGONQUIN PARK AREA
STANDS BURNED BEFORE LOGGING
(1100 plots)

Assoc.	Bal.	Y. bir.	H. maple	Hem.	W. spr.	B. spr.	W. pine
			Seedlings				
By–H	1993	851	3963	90	35	16	271
M–By	552	529	44,825	8	5	8	187
Pw–Bw	2309	1433	2267	51	23	16	328
By–B–S	672		400	8	16	32	112
Pw	1857				54	37	160
			Advance Growth				
By–H	112	19	12	39	6	1	
M–By	60	4	127	10	4		2
Pw–Bw	139	5	8	33	8	7	4
By–B–S	188	12	8		12	4	
Pw	506	1	2		8	21	59

ations of the Ottawa-Huron Region, is also important. To get clear results on the problem more work is necessary and this should include a study of the tolerant hardwoods.

9. Ogden, Price, Fripp, and Hillary Townships, 1941: *A. S. Michell*

Purpose
To determine the composition of young growth on these areas.

Area Studied
An area of 58,571 acres south and southwest of Timmins.
1. Soil and topography: Mostly sand, in some places shallow, overlying rock; flat or rolling. Hillary Township is more rugged with a sandy boulder clay soil.
2. Forest types: No attempt is made to classify the previous forest. Young growth is classed as conifer, hardwood, or mixedwood.
3. General conditions: Fires have occurred from 1912 to 1928 with varying intensities in virgin and cut-over stands and in places several times over the same area.

Method
Line plot method; lines across the topography, irregularly spaced but with intervals of at least ½ mile. Plots measured 100 feet × 11 feet (approximately 1/40 acre).
Observations were made of topography, ground cover, underbrush, age of burn from age of intolerant trees, soil, litter, and humus.
All trees and seedlings on the plots were tallied in 1″ d.b.h. classes, the lowest class including all under 0.5″ d.b.h. Diameter and height measurements were taken.
From these figures stand tables and percentage composition (from number of trees per acre) were calculated.
Composition figures do not always agree with type classification because types were taken from aerial photographs which give more prominence to dominant trees and less to very small seedlings.

Results and Conclusions
Table XVIII compiled from the data shows the composition of the present reproduction.
The following are the author's estimates of the eventual stand development.
Ogden Township: Will produce a jack pine timber crop, followed by a spruce pulpwood or a saw- and mining-timber crop.
Price Township: Present 16- to 23-year-old stands will at 90 to 100 years be similar to virgin stands further south on the same watershed (Grassy River).
Fripp Township: No forecast.
Hillary Township: The west half will be 20 per cent hardwood; 30 per cent partly commercial conifer swamp; remainder coniferous type, spruce predominating. The east half will be poor patchy mixedwood type.

TABLE XVIII

REPRODUCTION IN OGDEN, PRICE, FRIPP, AND HILLARY TOWNSHIPS

Township	No. plots	Percentage of total number of seedlings						Total seedlings per acre
		Pj	S	B	Po	Bw	Ce	
		Mixedwood type						
Ogden	68	38D	38	9	9D	6CoD		1421
Price	75	9D	18	39	15D	17D	2	1290
Fripp	206	6D	33	12	19D	28D	2	1277
Hillary		11D	59	17	2CoD	11CoD		2260
		Conifer type						
Price	97	37D	23	13	17CoD	7	3	1010
Fripp	20	28	52	4	6	10		1646

D—Dominant species; CoD—Co-dominants.

10. TIMAGAMI FOREST RESERVE, 1946: *H. C. Larsson*

Purpose

To study the condition of natural regeneration and planted stock in the reserved area bordering Timagami Lake and in the cut-over areas of Briggs and Strathcona townships.

Area Studied

Two areas were chosen for study: Tract A, situated on the north shore of the northeast arm of Lake Timagami in the townships of Briggs and Strathcona, and Tract B on the south shore in the Township of Briggs. The region in which the tracts are situated is in general flat and mostly covered with a mantle of glacial drift, consisting of sand interspersed with boulders and rocks. In spots a whitish silt layer 2–3 inches thick covers rock and sand. The region is drained by several small creeks originating in swamps. In both tracts the shore-lines and tops of the hills visible from the lake are reserved from cutting for scenic reasons; only dead and fallen trees are to be cut there.

The two tracts studied were evidently cut over between 1937 and 1941 for white pine, red pine, and white spruce. Early in the operation, clear cutting was practised; later, mature but defective seed trees were left. During logging operations the slash was piled and burned; the following spring or autumn the three commercial species were planted. Stock was from Midhurst, aged 2–4 years, planting density 74–300 trees per acre. Planting was confined to trails, roads, and skidways. No planting was done on very thin soils underlain by rock.

Method

Line plot system, with lines 400 feet apart. Plots were 400 feet apart, 1/20 acre in size, measuring 66 feet × 33 feet.

Observations and Conclusions

1. All species of regeneration, particularly the commercial species, are adversely affected by shrub growth.

2. Natural regeneration of the commercial species is very poor. White pine reproduction, although more abundant than red pine or white spruce, has poorer growth qualities owing to the effects of blister rust, weevil, and suppression by shrubbery.

3. In all cases the pine forest is mature or overmature. Average age in the reserved area on the north shore is 142 years, on the cut-over area 200 years. Defects average 0.4 per cent of the volume per year after 120 years.

4. Openings in the tree canopy (except on the thin soils) usually contain dense patches of hazel and mountain maple, interspersed with balsam, cedar, black spruce, and scattered poplar and white birch.

5. In some cases the planted stock is thriving and keeping ahead of the shrubbery; in other cases the shrubbery has already choked out or is now choking out the planted trees.

6. In the reserved area increment borings indicate that 50 per cent of the apparently healthy pine are defective.

7. The associations named "Pine," "Red Pine," and "Black Spruce Upland" are capable of natural pine regeneration if gradual thinnings are made.

8. White pine blister rust is widespread but sporadic on the cut-over area. It is most abundant on the wet areas or near water. It was not observed on trees greater than two inches in diameter nor on any trees on the reserved area.

9. Spruce budworm was active during the summer, defoliating considerable numbers of balsam of all sizes but evidently not affecting the spruce.

In the accompanying table (XIX) compiled from the report the associations capable of producing pine are shown.

Recommendations

Reserved areas

1. Periodic selective logging should be employed to remove overmature, defective, and suppressed trees.

2. Slash should be piled and burned.

3. Logging on shallow soils should coincide with seed years, but if natural regeneration is not successful within two or three years spot seeding is advised.

4. On deeper soils all gaps resulting from logging should be planted or seeded as soon as possible.

Unreserved areas

5. For shallow soils the same as (3).

6. On deeper soils planting should be continued when necessary, but on an experimental area of 1,000 acres or more try:

(a) vigorous seed trees left at four per acre or more.

(b) blocks of seed trees left at intervals of 200 feet, combined with live burning of slash and mechanical or chemical destruction of shrub growth.

TABLE XIX

ASSOCIATIONS CAPABLE OF PRODUCING PINE

(Split columns indicate figures for Tract A and Tract B respectively)

		Pine	Red pine	W. pine slope	W. pine flat	B. spruce upland
Area (acres)		1162	211	1795	317	35
Number of plots		222	37	335	60	8
Site		Well-drained slopes near rock ridges and outcrops	Rock ridges and outcrops and surrounding border	Well-drained, deep-soiled slopes	Deep-soiled, poorly drained valley bottoms with 1% slope	On moss cover on rock outcrops close to swamps
Original stand		Pr, Pw(Bw, Sw)	Pr(93%), Pw	Pw(90%), Pr(5%) (Ce, Sw, B)	B, Ce, Bw (Sw, Pw, By) .	Sb, B, Ce
Understory		B, Sb(Ce)	B, Sb(Ce, Pw)	B, Ce	Mm, Al, etc. (Sw)	
Present stand		B, Ce, Bw, Sb	B, Sb, Bw, Ce, Pw(Pr)	B, Ce, Sb, Bw, Sw, Pw	Unchanged	Unchanged
Regeneration by species (% of total)	Balsam	45 33	42 20	47 36	42 36	31
	Cedar	28 45	12 14	36 45	41 56	36
	B. spruce*	10 9	29 18	5 9	3 4	36
	W. spruce*	2 2	2 8	1 3	7	
	W. pine*	13 11	13 25	7 7	4 4	3
	R. pine*	1			1	
	W. birch	1 2	2 5	22 1	2	
Remarks		Dense shrubbery 13% 29%	Dense shrubbery on deeper soils	Shrubbery 40% 16%		Some windthrow from neighbouring cleared areas
% of plots with 500+ per acre reproduction	W. spruce	1 0	4 0	1 2	0 0	0
	W. pine	4 9	0 11	0 5	0 0	0
	R. pine	0 0	0 0	0 0	0 0	0

*In the Pine and the Red pine associations 10 per cent of the regeneration was planted, in the White pine slope and the White pine flat 90 per cent was planted.

General

7. White pine should be planted sparingly until effects of blister rust can be assessed.

8. Permanent sample plots should be established on all pine and white spruce sites to study the factors affecting growth and regeneration in the original stands and cut-over lands.

9. No extensive burning should be done on thin soils.

[In this report the material has been only partly condensed. Repetition of statements already made, splitting up of data, and the way in which the numerous tables are set up make it difficult to read the report with understanding.

The report contains a large amount of data which if properly presented would undoubtedly lend support to some of the conclusions reached by the author.]

11. THUNDER BAY REGION, 1946 (Part One of Research Report No. 14):
   H. C. Larsson

Purpose

To study the conditions of forest regeneration on cut-over and burnt-over land.

Area Studied

Four widely separate areas forming four distinct classes of forest were sampled. As a result, this represents four reports with a single introduction. Location of the four areas is as follows: Block I, drainage basin of the Black Sturgeon River, between Hurkett Ranger Station and Nonwatinose Lake; Block II, south shore of Lake Nipigon near Emerald Lake; Block III, east shore of Lake Nipigon on the Onaman River to Humbolt Bay; Block IV, near Long Lac and Little Long Lac.

The areas are situated in the Precambrian Shield, and are characterized by gentle slopes, flats, swamps, and scattered rock ridges; drainage is poor. Except on the uplands and rock cliffs the bed rock is overlain by unconsolidated glacial, lake, stream, and swamp deposits. The soils vary from fine sands and silty loams to coarse gravels, and are generally acid with a low nutrient content.

Method

Line plot system. Lines 400 feet apart. Plots of four sizes:
   *1/1000 acre— 6.6 feet × 6.6 feet
   1/40 acre—33 feet × 33 feet
   1/20 acre—66 feet × 33 feet
   1 acre

[*Here the plots (quadrats) were taken at intervals of 50 feet; occurrence of conifers was recorded for each quadrat; the number of conifers by species was apparently taken on every second quadrat. A complete tally (all species) and plot description were recorded every five hundred feet.]

Observations and Conclusions

1. Stands are generally even-aged (70–140 years), resulting from fires 60 to 170 years ago. A few individual white spruce between 140 and 170 years occur.

2. Probable succession on uncut land (as indicated by regeneration) is:

Present Stand	Site	Succession
Spruce–fir	Slopes, flats, swamps	Fir–spruce
Black spruce	Swamps, uplands	Present stand climax
Jack pine	Sand and gravel	Fir–spruce direct or
Red and white pine	Sand	via spruce–fir
		Fir–spruce

3. Uncut stands are generally healthy except balsam and white spruce in Blocks I and II which were severely attacked by spruce budworm.

4. On cut stands, seed trees are either unmerchantable species or cull defective specimens of merchantable species.

5. Over 80 per cent of the reproduction occurred during or prior to logging.

6. Slash and windfall covers 10–17 per cent of cutover, effectively preventing reproduction. Over twenty years is required for decomposition of the slash.

[In this report percentage figures have been used excessively and the splitting up of data could have been reduced to advantage. Unfortunately some of the table headings are obscure in meaning; for example, "Percent Reproduction per Acre" refers to the number of seedlings per acre based on the list plots, but "Percent Reproduction" refers to the percentage of occurrences on the stocking plots. It is therefore difficult to read the report with understanding.]

12. WESTERN REGION, 1946 (Part Two of Research Report No. 14):
G. C. Wilkes

Purpose

To study quantity and composition of reproduction on cut-over areas.

Area Studied

Twenty-two cut-over areas were sampled in the Lake of the Woods Pulp Concession of the Ontario-Minnesota Pulp and Paper Company. The areas are, for the most part, near the Heenan Highway south of Kenora within the Precambrian Shield. The terrain is marked by low rock ridges interspersed with small lakes and swamps. The soils are generally shallow except in the flats and swamps.

Cutting for pulp, lumber, and ties extended over the period 1926–46.

Method

The same as that used for the Thunder Bay region (see No. 11, above).

Observations and Conclusions

1. Stocking of regeneration appears "moderate."

2. Balsam reproduction predominates on well-drained sites, followed by that of spruce, cedar, white birch, and trembling aspen.

3. In the swamps black spruce and white cedar regeneration predominates in the cuts made since 1936, but balsam predominates in the older cuts.

4. Pines are not reproducing appreciably.

5. Between 75 and 90 per cent of the total reproduction is ¼ inch or less in diameter, and of this, one-half is in the ½ foot height class.

6. Jack pine residuals are in poor condition because of insect attack. Some larch sawfly damage is evident. Blister rust was observed on white pine reproduction.

7. Seed trees appear to be present in sufficient quantities.

[In this report the table headings are not always clear and in some cases it is difficult to deduce quantitative results from the tables. Number of plots taken has not been stated. Percentage figures are used excessively; for example, number of seedlings per acre of various species would be better left as such—to show them again in percentages is not helpful. The figures given to show numbers per acre have not been derived for the same time periods as the stocking figures; therefore one cannot determine both distribution and quantity for a given species within a given type.]

13. Spruce Falls Power and Paper Company, Limited
Research Report No. 10 (Revised), 1947: *R. C. Hosie*

[This survey of regeneration was a co-operative study sponsored by the University of Toronto, the Department of Lands and Forests, and the Spruce Falls Power and Paper Company. Since it reveals conditions on the limits of that company it is reviewed in the section covering their reports.]

14. Midwestern and Western Regions, 1947
(Part One of Research Report No. 17): *H. C. Larsson*

Purpose

To continue the study of forest regeneration on cut-over and burned-over land in the midwestern and western regions of Ontario.

Area Studied

Block A, west of the Trans-Canada Highway between Raith and Linko near Savanne Lake (2 square miles);

Block B, at Valora between Surprise and Wintering Lakes (2 square miles);

Block C, along both sides of the "lower" Pic River for about 20 miles from the mouth (5 square miles).

Soil conditions are similar to those indicated in Larsson's Thunder Bay report of 1946 (*see* No. 11, above).

Method

Line plot system. Lines 200 feet apart in areas of 100 acres or less, and 400 feet apart in larger areas. Plots 1/1000 acre, measuring 6.6 feet square. In Blocks A and B, the occurrence of conifers was recorded every 50 feet, in Block C occurrence and the number of all species were counted every 50 feet. In both cases a complete reproduction tally by size classes was made every 500 feet. Scattered 1/20-acre plots were used to study past and present forest cover types.

Observations and Conclusions

1. The original forest is composed of both uneven-aged and even-aged stands, most merchantable stands being between 80 and 120 years old.

2. Balsam is generally 15 to 37 years younger than the other merchantable species.

3. Ninety per cent of the coniferous reproduction occurs before or during cutting.

4. Cutting stimulates asexual regeneration of poplar and white birch.

5. Uncut stands which experience a single fire are usually regenerated to black spruce, jack pine, poplar, and white birch. These occur in about the same proportions as they did in the original stands.

6. Burned cut-over lands do not usually reproduce to conifer species. Scattered patches of poplar and white birch come in on the better soils; no reproduction comes in in the swamps.

7. Moist loams and clay silts are generally covered with dense competitive vegetation one or two years after the fire. Sandy soils and black spruce swamps may remain free of competitive growth for ten years after a burn.

8. Spruce regeneration of different ages occurs most abundantly on the extreme sites: the swamps and the dry soils. Balsam is the predominant species on the intermediate sites.

9. No evidence of serious damage by fungi or insects was found.

10. Percentage of plots stocked is as follows:

	Spruce	Balsam	Either
Block A	38	33	62
Block B	28	44	62
Block C	19	32	43
All	26	36	54

11. Percentage of plots stocked by cutting periods (Blocks A and B) is as follows:

	Spruce	Balsam	Either
Cut within the last five years	27	36	56
Cut five to twenty years ago	46	46	77
Factor of increase	1.70	1.28	1.38

[Some of the conclusions reached by the author of this report are of particular interest, for example, that 90 per cent of the coniferous reproduction occurs before and not after logging and that cutting stimulates asexual regeneration of poplar and white birch. Unfortunately there is no supporting evidence given, but there has been a noticeable tendency in the later reports of the Department to stress the preponderance of advance growth over reproduction since logging.]

15. WESTERN REGION, 1947 (Part Two of Research Report No. 17):
N. F. Lyon

Purpose
To continue the studies of forest regeneration in the western region of Ontario.

Area Studied
Block I, north shore of Black Sturgeon Lake in Pettypiece Township (three areas); Block II, northeast shore of Canon Lake (one area); Block III, north shore of Atikwa Lake (two areas); Block IV, Mafeking Township (two areas); Block V, on the Trans-Canada Highway between Dinorwic and Dyment (five areas).
The terrain is rough and rolling, interspersed with numerous rocky-shored lakes. Soils are chiefly gravel, sand, loam, and clay silt.

Method
The same as that outlined in Larsson's report on the midwestern and western regions (see No. 14, above).

Observations and Conclusions
1. After cutting, stands reproduce as follows:
(*a*) Spruce-balsam to balsam and trembling aspen.
(*b*) Spruce swamps to spruce.
(*c*) Jack pine to spruce-balsam, or balsam–aspen–white birch.
2. Burning of slash in jack pine cutovers during the spring following cutting seemed to increase the amount of jack pine reproduction.
3. Stocking of reproduction seemed to improve with the passage of time following a cut, as the following table tends to show:

Block	Cutting period	Stocking of reproduction
I	6–15 years ago	Moderate
II	1– 5 years ago	Understocked to failure
III	6–15 years ago	Good
IV	1– 5 years ago	Understocked
V	11–20 years ago	Good

[The assumption that stocking improves with age following cutting because the older cut-over areas are better stocked than those more recently cut is faulty. It could be just a coincidence that the poorly stocked areas are those most recently cut over. Also, there is the probability that the older cut-over areas were logged less severely than more recent ones, and that they were old stands at the time of cutting. In either case a greater amount of advance growth would be left after logging.]

16. THE GOGAMA FIRE (1941), 1948: *D. H. Burton*

Purpose

To determine the present condition of the reproduction as to stocking and health.

Method

The line plot method and ocular estimation. In the case of the former, mil-acre quadrats spaced 100 feet apart on the line being run were tallied for all tree species by height classes. For the ocular estimate, lines 4 to 5 miles in length were run for mapping purposes and at the same time notes were made on the presence or absence of regeneration, age of seedlings, underbrush and ground cover, and type of soil. Aerial photographs were used to determine the line locations. A three-man party was employed for two months.

Observations

Three types, based mainly on the original stand, are referred to and briefly described: Jack pine; mixedwood—jack pine, poplar, birch, red and white pine; spruce and black ash swamps.

In the jack pine type, regeneration is almost pure jack pine, and in general, whether the stands were cut or uncut before the burn, the type is now adequately stocked. White birch seedlings were not found and the percentage of this species is less in the new stand than previously. Spruce, balsam, and poplar are sparse.

In the mixedwood type, the stands that were uncut previous to the burn are not now adequately stocked to any species, whereas the areas cut before the fire appear to be adequately stocked to both jack pine and hardwoods. Areas that previously had an admixture of white and red pine are not reproducing to these species, and it is unlikely that these two species will be represented in the future stands.

The fire occurred in May, and in all probability did not do very great damage to the underbrush which has taken over and is hindering the development of seedlings.

[This survey was a rapid reconnaissance largely intended as a means of making an approximate map for management purposes showing areas where regeneration definitely is, or is not, satisfactory; it was not a regeneration survey of the usual type.]

17. IROQUOIS FALLS, 1948 (Research Report No. 16): *D. H. Burton*

Purpose

To relocate and tally 48 permanent sample plots that were established in 1925 by the Abitibi Power and Paper Company on certain cut-over areas near the Company railway. The plots were established for the purpose of determining whether or not the cutting methods practised by the Company were being followed by adequate regeneration. The present report combines the essential data of the work of both 1925 and 1947.

Method

The three-man party was able to locate 43 of the 48 plots, which measure 100 × 100 feet. On relocation, tie posts and plot corner posts were renewed and a complete tally of all the species was taken. Seedlings were recorded in height classes and trees above 0.5 inches d.b.h. were calipered or measured with a diameter tape. Where ground cover was too thick for an accurate tally of the seedlings on the plot, several one-square-foot spot checks were made. All plots were check tallied. A description of each plot was made and soil samples of each were taken for analysis.

To determine the ages of the seedlings recorded, three seedlings per height class were taken just off the plot and age counts of them made with the aid of a hand lens. The ages obtained for each height class were averaged. The assumption was then made that all seedlings within a given height class were approximately that average age. The established classes are:

	Spruce swamp type	Mixedwood
Class I—0 to 0.5 feet	7 years	7 years
Class II—0.5 to 1.5 feet	10 ”	10 ”
Class III—1.6 to 2.5 feet	15 ”	16 ”
Class IV—2.6 feet to 0.5 inches d.b.h.	20 ”	20 ”

Observations

Two cover types, the black spruce swamp and the mixedwood, are dealt with. Of the 43 plots located, 17 are referred to the former and 11 to the latter. For various reasons the other plots are ruled out as being untypical.

There has been a decrease in the number of spruce per plot (ranging from 19 to 79 per cent) between the years 1925 and 1947, except in the case of three plots. This downward trend is considered normal.

The established seedling classes reveal that from 35 to 52 per cent of the present tree stand has seeded in since the cut.

For the spruce swamps the counts show a moderate stocking of spruce and in the mixedwood a favourable stocking of balsam which predominates over all other species. Black spruce is not reproducing to an appreciable extent on the slopes, whereas previous to cutting it formed a large percentage of the stand. In general the reproduction is healthy except for damage to balsam from the spruce budworm.

Table XX shows the tally for spruce and balsam for 1925 and 1947. The data were taken from summary tables 1 and 2 in the report.

[It is difficult to accept the observation that from 35 to 52 per cent of the present tree stand on the plots has seeded in since the cut. The figures on which the statement is based are estimates which may or may not be correct. Seeding-in following logging is of great importance on areas at present understocked and it is unfortunate that an exact determination of this important development was not made on at least a small part of each plot taken.]

TABLE XX

TALLY FOR SPRUCE AND BALSAM 1925 AND 1947, IROQUOIS FALLS

Plot No.	Total number per plot (all ages) 1925	1947	Estimated number seeded in since cut	Year of cut
		Spruce		
1	582	*300	63	1924–25
2	860	215	101	"
3	1064	520	272	"
4	587	395	138	"
12	126	41	12	1923–24
15	527	871	316	1922–23
17	634	157	85	1914–15
18	970	639	433	1919–20
20	1068	534	268	1921–22
25	876	184	55	1920–21
26	453	167	66	1918–19
28	748	384	169	1921–22
29	351	356	237	1924–25
30	234	159	117	1924–25
31	326	250	155	1924–25
34	547	599	478	1924–25
47	169	138	20	1917–18
	10,122	5909	2965	
		Balsam		
6	658	707	324	1924–25
7	412	665	388	"
9	645	397	152	"
10	624	787	310	"
11	610	542	334	"
21	895	979	655	1921–22
27	529	754	587	1918–19
35	444	210	58	1924–25
37	1725	382	190	"
38	664	259	100	"
39	1633	653	241	"
	8839	6333	3339	

*1947 totals include number seeded in.

18. MIDWESTERN REGION (Section One of Research Report No. 19), 1949: H. C. Larsson and N. F. Lyon

Purpose

To assess the effect of mechanical logging, spring burning of slash, chemical poisoning of stands, and budworm infestation on pulpwood repro-duction.

Area Studied
The vicinity of Stevens referred to as Block D and an area near the south-west corner of Black Sturgeon Lake, Block E. Both areas are situated within the Precambrian Shield. Topography is quite varied; the underlying rock is covered with thick glacial and post-glacial deposits.

Method
Sample areas were located from Company maps and reconnoitred by a two-man party before sampling. Permanent sample plots were established in certain of these areas. Mil-acre quadrats taken in groups of ten were used to record the regeneration on the permanent sample plots. On larger tracts where permanent plots were not established, the line plot method of sampling was used with mil-acre quadrats at 50-foot intervals on lines 100 feet apart, or 200 feet apart on areas of 200 or more acres.

Observations
1. The following table taken from page 9 in the report shows the percentages of mil-acre quadrats stocked to balsam, spruce, and jack pine reproduction in the uncut stands examined.

Forest cover site type	*Number of quadrats*	*B*	*S*	*Pj*	*B and S*	*S and Pj*	*B or S or Pj*
Poplar slope (poisoned)*	100	45	1	0	2	0	48
Poplar slope	174	59	1	0	3	0	63
Poplar–conifer slope	58	52	9	0	5	0	66
Jack pine–poplar–spruce slope	100	18	41	0	2	0	61
Jack pine–spruce slope	200	3	65	0	3	<1	71
Jack pine slope	260	1	13	2	<1	0	16
Black spruce plot	100	9	22	0	1	0	32

*Ammonium sulphamate, arsenic-ammonium sulphamate, and 2-4-D were used to kill the tree stand prior to cutting. These poisons were applied in paste form in a narrow girdle made on the trees at approximately 2 feet above the ground.

2. Reproduction on mechanically logged areas within one year of operations is as follows:

Forest cover type	*Number of quadrats*	*Percentage of quadrats stocked to B or S or Pj*
Poplar–conifer slope	375	42
Jack pine slope (winter operation)	245	5
Jack pine slope (summer operation)	280	18

A number of observations and conclusions regarding the effect of mechanical logging on regeneration are given, amongst them the following:
(a) Cotyledonous reproduction did occur following logging.
(b) All one-year-old seedlings found were jack pine. Areas winter logged were complete failures.

(c) Areas summer logged showed considerable cotyledonous jack pine.

(d) Cotyledonous jack pine were found only on exposed mineral soil.

(e) Advance growth suffered considerably during logging, 12 to 23 per cent of the advance growth being destroyed.

(f) Mechanical logging prepares the sites better for regeneration than all other logging methods so far observed.

3. Reproduction following slash burning is indicated in a table reporting the percentage of mil-acre quadrats stocked to balsam, spruce, and jack pine reproduction in unburned and burned-over jack pine cutovers.

Condition	Number of quadrats	B only	S only	Pj only	B or S or Pj
Unburned	116	3	20	1	24
Burned	223	1	1	1	4

Eight observations are made and amongst the conclusions are the following:

(a) A light slash fire during early spring following logging operations when the ground is saturated with moisture is unsuccessful as an agent in restocking a cutover to conifers.

(b) Observations of both natural and artificially set fires indicated that the most important prerequisites for successful regeneration following fires are as follows: (1) seed trees; (2) abundance of viable seed; (3) complete burning of the litter and humus; (4) adequate precipitation during the growing season.

4. Some stands were chemically poisoned with arsenic, ammonium sulphamate, arsenic-ammonium sulphamate, and 2-4-D.

Occurrence of reproduction in healthy and poisoned stands is given as the following percentages:

	Number of quadrats	B	S	Bw	A
Healthy stand	174	62	4	1	2
Poisoned stand	100	47	3	0	18

It was concluded that

(a) None of the poisons have any immediate detrimental effects on regeneration when applied during the months of June, July, August, and September.

(b) Treated trees appear to be able to transmit the poison to untreated grafts and layerings.

(c) Animal and bird life was not noticeably affected.

5. The study of reproduction in an uncut budworm-infested forest was undertaken in Block E. The area had been heavily infested with spruce budworm for the previous four years.

Occurrence of reproduction is given in percentages in Table XXI.

Recommendations

1. All cutting operations on timber limits should be so laid out that the mature, overmature, and unhealthy stands can be harvested before they become a total economic loss.

TABLE XXI

REPRODUCTION IN UNCUT BUDWORM INFESTED FOREST,
BLACK STURGEON AREA, 1949

Transect no.	No. quadrats	B %	S %	A %	Ce %
	uncut poplar-conifer slope				
1	100	57	8	23	0
2	100	79	14	28	1
	uncut conifer slope				
3	100	68	21	7	
	black spruce flat				
4	100	34	19	1	0
	black spruce swamp				
5	100	30	70	0	0
6	100	39	54	0	0
7	100	85	46	0	5

2. Greater utilization of merchantable trees should be encouraged by both government and company personnel.

3. Experimental studies should be conducted on various logging methods and wage systems to determine which gives the best results, not only for production, but also from the standpoint of utilization and silviculture.

4. Companies should be equipped so that they can log and utilize all merchantable species.

5. Cutters should be paid a bonus on a cordage or on an acreage basis for fulfilling certain silvicultural obligations deemed necessary by both government and company foresters for the benefit of the future crop and for fuller utilization of the present crop.

6. Bush workers and logging camps should be utilized not only for logging but also as a means of conducting any silvicultural treatment thought necessary for the establishment of the next crop.

7. Regeneration studies should be conducted in the main forest cover site types immediately before and after operations to determine the percentage loss of advance growth by the various logging methods.

8. Planting or other forms of silvicultural treatment to increase future yields and to improve the quality of the next crop should be conducted wherever necessary as soon as possible after logging operations.

9. Considerable time and thought should be spent on developing silvicultural equipment which can operate in a mechanical fashion on cut-over and burned-over land.

10. Silvicultural studies should be conducted on recently burned-over land to determine methods of restocking devastated areas.

11. Experimental aerial and ground seeding using naked and pelleted seeds should be continued on recent burns.

12. Slash burning should never be conducted as a silvicultural practice to promote regeneration unless it is done on an experimental scale.

13. Fire should be kept out of all cut-over areas as it destroys most of the regeneration and seed trees.

14. All forest regions should have good facilities for the gathering, extracting, treating, and storing of tree seed.

[These studies are of a preliminary nature and conclusions drawn are only tentative. They perhaps mark the beginning of efforts to develop methods of obtaining natural reproduction following disturbances.]

19. WESTERN REGION (Section Two of Research Report No. 19), 1949: G. W. Cameron

Purpose

To determine if cut-over areas are being adequately restocked, particularly with red and white pine, and also to determine where possible the effects of various factors on pine reproduction.

Area Studied

The Fort Frances District. Work was restricted to white and red pine stands cut 5 to 8 years ago.

Method

Line plot system. Two sizes of plots: mil-acre plots (6.6 feet $\times$ 6.6 feet) at 50-foot intervals for recording numbers and distribution of the reproduction; 1/20 acre plots (66 feet $\times$ 33 feet) at intervals of 500 feet to determine past and present cover types. Lines 200 feet apart.

Results

The following figures show the percentage of mil-acre quadrats stocked to reproduction on the different cut-over land encountered:

Type	Number of quadrats	Pw	Pr	B	S	Bw	Po
Pine (R & W)	59	57	12	18	0	12	6
Pine–hardwood slope	83	18	12	35	4	12	16
White pine upland	51	29	0	29	15	0	15
Red pine upland	588	32	5	32	7	6	9
Red pine slope	97	21	6	42	16	22	13
Red pine–spruce upland	79	15	1	16	14	2	28
Red pine–hardwood slope	668	28	7	38	6	15	14
Red pine–spruce– hardwood upland	40	7	1	25	17	3	7
Red pine–spruce– hardwood slope	66	7	3	29	17	9	20

Conclusions

1. Regeneration was moderately successful in all cut-over areas examined.

2. White pine seedlings frequently occurred in clumps on rotting logs. Thus reproduction in numbers per acre gives a more pleasing picture than do the stocking percentages.

3. Height-age study of seedlings indicated that most of the pine regeneration came in during and immediately following the cutting operations.

4. Underbrush was rarely sufficiently dense to hinder the establishment of regeneration.

[The stocking percentages given for the different species on different types are based, in all but two cases, on insufficient samples to give reliable figures. In the two cases for which a large number of quadrats were taken, namely red pine upland and red pine–hardwood slope, the stocking for white pine is approximately 30 per cent. This stocking is probably higher than that on many other cut-over pine areas in the Province and might indicate a tendency for better white pine reproduction in parts of the Fort Frances District than in Timagami, Algonquin Park, and other parts of Ontario.]

NATIONAL RESEARCH COUNCIL

1. WHITE PINE SUCCESSION AS INFLUENCED BY FIRE, 1941: *K. M. Mayall*

Purpose

To ascertain the present condition of white pine regeneration, to chart the probable succession in the chief types containing white pine, to rate particularly the significance of fire, and to make recommendations for improved management.

Areas Studied

Seven widely distributed areas on both sides of the Ottawa River: Little Nipissing River; Opeongo River; Crow River; Madawaska; Deep River, Quebec; Timagami; Petawawa Forest Experiment Station.

Method

Field work was preceded by a review of the literature on white pine, particularly reports of previous regeneration surveys. This literature was summarized and provided the information on which the report is mainly based. Apparently the field work consisted of personal inspection by the author to determine developments in the above areas since the writing of the reports that were reviewed.

Observations

Seven reports were analysed and significant features of each given. (Only those features for the reports not reviewed above are given here.)

(i) *Growth Conditions in the Forests of Algonquin Park*, 1929; Forestry Branch, Canada, W. M. Robertson (No. 4).

(ii) *Regeneration of Cut-over Pine Lands, Algonquin Park*, 1931; Department of Lands and Forests, A. P. Leslie (No. 6).

(iii) *Cut-over Pine Lands, North Bay Inspectorate*, 1930; Department of Lands and Forests (No. 3).

(iv) *Beauchene River Survey*, 1935; D. K. Maissurov (probably a survey made by the Forestry Branch, Canada). Six hundred square miles of the Beauchene watershed near Mattawa were surveyed. The area was formerly 70 per cent softwood, chiefly red and white pine, only about 5 per cent restocked with white pine, all originating after fires. Management recommended is clear cutting and slash burning in a seed year, with dependence on the adjacent stand for seed.

(v) *Growth Conditions in the Forests of Gatineau and Lièvre Watersheds*, 1929–30; Forestry Branch, Canada, W. M. Robertson. Reports a fair amount of white pine in the maturing age classes and very little reproduction.

(vi) *Rate of Growth Survey, Sudbury District*, 1939; Forestry Branch, Canada, G. A. Mulloy. Reports white pine reproduction as being negligible in most sub-types.

(vii) *Lower Gatineau Woodlands Survey*, 1935; Forestry Branch, Canada,

W. M. Robertson. Reports area has changed from red and white pine to almost pure hardwood.

Observations on the areas inspected were:

1. *Little Nipissing River.* A plateau on which a white pine stand, 88 trees per acre, 135 years old, was partly cut in 1929. Slash covered 25 per cent of the area. Aspen and other reproduction was dense. Within 150 yards of the uncut stand there were 330 white pine seedlings per acre. In the centre of the cut, with 1 seed tree per 4 acres, there were 50 white pine seedlings per acre. Seeding took place one year after cutting.

The remainder of the plateau, cut over in 1938, a good seed year, showed advance growth of only 5 seedlings per acre.

The hardwood type averaged less than 1 white pine tree per acre, and seedlings were negligible.

Two sand flats in the cut-over area and one in the uncut show no adequate regeneration.

2. *Opeongo River.* Stands from 200 to 250 years old, almost pure pine, were cut in 1931–3; they had been burned moderately in 1924, and parts were burned again later. White pine seedlings were fewer than 20 per acre, but were found near every seed tree. One slope showed 230 seedlings per acre. Tolerant hardwood hills were unburned and contained little or no pine.

3. *Crow River.* Uncut white pine stands 350 years old were still producing an adequate seed supply, but lacked advance growth.

4. *Madawaska.* The area examined had been frequently burned; it was almost free of humus, with low water table. Second growth white pine numbered 2 or 3 per square mile; seedlings were absent.

5. *Deep River, Quebec.* Lower slopes are aspen white pine type. Cutting in 1914 produced no pine regeneration. Recutting in 1937 produced 60 white pine seedlings per acre. Pine on cliffs and talus slopes give continued seed supply, and cutting of poplar may favour white pine reproduction.

6. *Timagami.* Former clear cutting resulted in about 50 white pine seedlings per acre. Present methods, with slash lopped or burned and faulty trees left, produce about 200 seedlings per acre. White pine–yellow birch lowlands between Timagami and North Bay have inadequate regeneration, and planting of pine is being done by the Department of Lands and Forests to bring the amount up to 300 per acre.

Insufficient seed trees and dense spruce-fir advance growth seem to be critical factors.

7. *Petawawa Forest Experiment Station.* Not enough is known yet to estimate mortality in immature mixedwood stands. Heavy thinning of a plot of 50-year-old pine resulted in 700 seedlings per acre. The removal of pine and some hardwoods from a mixedwood stand increased regeneration from an average of 125 per acre to an average of 350 per acre.

Conclusions and Recommendations

The author concludes that both burned and unburned cut-over lands suffer from lack of seed trees, that the maximum reproduction without fire to remove tolerant species will be 300 to 400 white pine seedlings per acre, and that such regeneration will probably not give more than 30 mature trees per acre. Burning stimulates regeneration in old pine stands, but its use in cut-over younger stands is of doubtful value.

He states that we have insufficient information on germination and growth on burned and unburned soils, the effect of white pine weevil in retarding the development of dominance, the seriousness of blister rust, the most advantageous degree and season of burning, the minimum number of seed trees required, and mortality in young stands.

Further work is recommended to determine the relationship of seed years to regeneration. Re-examination of surveyed areas and the use of permanent sample plots are considered the only methods for obtaining a reliable estimate of the number of seedlings needed to provide a final crop.

ABITIBI POWER AND PAPER COMPANY, LIMITED

Studies in forest regeneration by the Abitibi Power and Paper Company began in 1919 when, in co-operation with the Commission of Conservation of that time, the first regeneration study in Ontario was made (see Forestry Branch, Canada, report no. 1, p. 38 above). Until 1928, when the Spanish River Pulp and Paper Company was taken over by Abitibi, experimental work was carried out independently by each company, Spanish River experiments being confined to the Sault Ste Marie, and Abitibi experiments to the Iroquois Falls, areas. All experimental work was abandoned in 1930 owing to the general business depression then prevailing.

Following the war, the present Abitibi Company began the re-establishment of its work in forest research in 1946. In August, 1949, a silvicultural field meeting of the Canadian Pulp and Paper Association was held at Iroquois Falls. For the information of the delegates at that meeting, several reports were prepared by different members of the Company which describe briefly the experimental work carried out to date. Six of these dealt with or had reference to forest regeneration, and are included in this review.

Although one of these reports (No. 2) recommends that a twenty mil-acre quadrat plot be adopted as the standard for regeneration surveys, the author of that report now advises that equally satisfactory results at lower cost can be obtained by using mil-acre quadrats spaced at one-chain intervals with a complete count every tenth quadrat. If the interval between quadrats is paced, such a survey can be carried out by one man.

1. Nurseries and Plantations, 1949: *O. G. Larsson*

Purpose

This paper describes briefly the results of two experimental nurseries in operation between 1920 and 1928 and the experience gained from plantation work carried on from 1922 to 1927.

Nurseries

The first nursery was established at Twin Falls on an area with heavy clay soil—a site typical of the northern Clay Belt, and therefore considered suitable for the experiment. Approximately nine acres were marked out and cleared in the autumn of 1919. In 1920, after soil preparation, the first seed was sown. Seed of Norway and white spruce was mainly used, but some black spruce, sitka spruce, balsam, and tamarack seed was also sown. Of 1,350,000 seedlings obtained, the majority were heaved out the following spring, and an attempt to prevent this happening again was made by ploughing a mixture of sand and black muck into the 1921 seedbeds. This did not prevent heaving, and a second nursery was chosen on a sand plain about four and one-half miles farther north.

The soil of this second nursery was a fine white sand, slightly acid, over-lying a coarser yellow sand and having good drainage.

Observation of this nursery disclosed that it was satisfactory and would, if given normal nursery attention, be successful. However, during the period 1924 to 1927 no new seedbeds were begun, the work being confined to lifting stock for outplanting, transplanting, and tending. In 1928 the nursery project was abandoned.

Plantations

The first outplanting, done in 1922, consisted of 11,000 Norway spruce from an outside nursery, set out in 10 small plots. In 1923, 2000 jack pine and 2000 Scots pine were taken from the abandoned Twin Falls Nursery and planted around the second nursery. These have all died since that time. Additional planting was done in 1924, 1925, 1926, and 1927. Altogether 38 separate plantations were made, comprising 384 acres and using slightly over 467,000 trees. With the exception of two plots (Nos. 19 and 20 on sand) all the planting was on heavy well-drained clay. In 1948 a study of these plantings revealed that 78 per cent of the original stock was dead, 9 per cent cull, and 13 per cent satisfactory.

The reasons for such high mortality are given as: (a) damage done by the varying hare during 1924–5, one of its population peaks; (b) horses grazing; (c) drought; (d) insects; (e) fungi; (f) frost.

Conclusions

It is stated that the two experiments, although now classed as unsuccess-ful, have yielded a great deal of valuable information with regard to: (a) features necessary in a nursery site; (b) nursery treatment; (c) per-formance of species; (d) spacing for outplanting; (e) plantation sites for various species; (f) particular enemies of various species; (g) relative growth of various species.

Periodic studies of the outplantings are being continued.

2. REPRODUCTION OF PULPWOOD STANDS, 1949: *A. R. McKenzie*

Purpose

This paper is based on an examination of four reports and the observations of the writer. The reports referred to are:

(i) Research Report No. 10 (revised), 1947; Ontario Department of Lands and Forests, R. C. Hosie.

(ii) Research Report No. 16, 1948; Ontario Department of Lands and Forests, D. H. Burton.

(iii) Progress Report, Reproduction Survey, Cochrane District Section B-4, 1948; Forestry Branch, R. H. Candy.

(iv) The Silvicultural Research Program of the Spruce Falls Power and Paper Company; C.P.P.A. Woodlands Section Index 1006; E. Bonner.

Observations

(Only those with reference to cut-over areas are included here.)

1. All studies conducted in the Cochrane district show that, if cut-over lands are protected from fire damage, they will restock with sufficient spruce-balsam reproduction to ensure an adequate second cut.

2. The percentage of spruce regeneration falls sharply as drainage improves, varying from 100 per cent black spruce on the semi-muskeg site to a 25 per cent stocking or less on the best drained sites.

3. Accurate predictions are impossible but it can be assumed that, at the best, the proportion of spruce in the next cut will not exceed the spruce content of the original stands and that, particularly on the better drained sites, the percentage of balsam will in many cases be greatly increased. The possibility of future budworm damage is thus a serious hazard.

4. The cut-over areas in the vicinity show a lack of uniformity, being extremely patchy.

5. A noticeable feature of the district is the heavy alder growth, particularly on the wet flats.

6. There is a need for making all existing data on forest regeneration available to some permanent central agency where they can be recorded, correlated, and analysed.

7. The twenty quadrat plot should be adopted as the standard for regeneration surveys. The interval between plots or between strips can be varied.

8. There is a need for the establishment of a uniform terminology. Suggested definitions for some of the common terms are given.

9. A short discussion on the time that should lapse between the disturbance (cutting or fire) and the survey suggests a period of ten years on cutovers and fifteen years on burned areas.

10. In a short discussion on the question of successful reproduction it is pointed out that no one as yet knows what degree of spruce-balsam stocking is required in the first twenty years to ensure a satisfactory second cut at maturity. The recommendation is made that the stocking standards of the Forestry Branch be adopted until such time as a better standard is available.

11. The conclusion is given that all indications are that some reproduction is established after the cut, but if sufficient stems survive the cut to produce re-stocking, these young seedlings will be killed by suppression or, if established in openings, will not have reached merchantable size by the time the stand as a whole is ready for the second cut.

12. In a discussion on the question of improving the content of spruce-balsam reproduction on cut-over areas, two steps are suggested: (a) whenever possible, confine cutting to mature stands where a good crop of natural reproduction is already established; (b) preserve this reproduction by reducing logging damage to a minimum.

The report concludes with an outline of the company's silvicultural programme.

[This paper emphasizes many of the matters that are of first importance in carrying out forest regeneration studies, among them: the standardization of survey methods, the establishment of a uniform terminology, the determination of stocking standards, a means of separating advance growth from reproduction since cutting, the time when cut-over areas should be surveyed. These are matters that have given rise to some confusion in the minds of investigators and to some misunderstandings in the interpretation of data presented in reports.]

3. Mace Bay, Iroquois Falls, 1949: *K. W. Carlisle*

Purpose

An experiment to prove or disprove the economy of moving logs from the stump to the haul road by mechanical means and the effect of such an operation on the reproduction.

Observations

1. It is thought that since the mechanical operation of dragging logs in bunches exposes mineral soil it should be favourable to the germination of black spruce seeds. Winter yarding would be ineffective in exposing this soil.

2. The damage done to advance growth by a mechanical operation is not as severe as that done by horse logging, mainly because of the narrower road used and a less thorough clearing.

[The observations made are not based on recorded data, and must therefore be accepted with caution.]

4. Sault Ste Marie Division, 1949: *B. J. Smith*

Purpose

To outline the silvicultural work which has been carried out by the Company at the Sault Ste Marie Division.

Permanent Sample Plots

One 1-acre plot was established in 1925 in a 70-year-old spruce-balsam wet flat site near Carp Creek, 4 miles west of the Sault mill. Remeasured in 1948, the plot shows that 80 of the 334 trees left after cutting in 1925 have survived. The present reproduction consists of a dense stand of young balsam up to 4 inches d.b.h. and 25 feet tall. Spruce that had been planted in 1926 did not survive, owing apparently to the good natural reproduction suppressing it.

In the Bouchard Lake area near Regan two plots were established in the winter of 1948–9 to determine (*a*) if a preliminary cut for hardwood will effect the amount of coniferous regeneration established, (*b*) the effect on coniferous regeneration of cutting black spruce in various strip widths. Results are not expected for five years.

Nursery Work

The nursery site established in 1920 by the Spanish River Pulp and Paper Company and closed in 1930 is not now in use.

Forest Plantations
Planting was carried on from 1925 to 1930 on the Goulais River and Agawa River areas.

The Goulais River Plantation covers approximately 625 acres and originally contained over 800,000 trees (spruce) planted between 1925 and 1928. In 1949 this plantation was mapped from aerial photographs and subdivided into types on the basis of ground cover; three sample plots were established. Ground checks show there are now probably around 700 spruce per acre; the original planting was 1,200 to 1,400 per acre.

The Agawa River Plantation is made up of two plantings: 62,100 spruce planted in 1929—now classed as a success—and 161,000 trees planted in 1930—much less successful.

In the summary it is stated that even on the best sites the spruce that has died has not been killed by competition from other spruce or natural regeneration, but by drought or other causes, that the surviving spruce is healthy and growth has improved in recent years, and that the plantations as a whole may yet prove to be successful. It is considered that the relatively slow rate of growth to date is due to the fact that, with the possible exception of the 1929 Agawa planting, the sites planted are better adapted to pine than to spruce.

5. BRUSH DISPOSAL, 1949: *E. S. Groome*

Purpose
This experiment was carried out in 1928 to study the problem of disposing of brush and logging slash and all the various phases of such an operation, silvicultural, economic, operative and protective.

The area is located in Lot VI, Concession II, Stimson Township, north of the Canadian National Railway and west of mileage 18 on the Abitibi Railway. The forest is of the black spruce swamp type.

Method
The experiment was carried out on four 5-acre plots and one 10-acre plot. Each plot was cruised for a tally of the sizes of each species, living, diseased, and dead. Notes were made on the logging conditions, drainage, topography and vegetation.

Logging was done on all six plots by the usual method employed by the company, namely cut and bunch. Log lengths were 16 feet. This system involves parallel strips 40 to 50 feet wide. Through the middle of each, a rough road is made which leads to the main haul roads. The cutters work singly, one to a strip, felling the trees parallel to the road, bucking them into log lengths, then moving the logs by hand into piles of 15 to 50 logs alongside the strip road. Tops and branches are left where they fall in the strip, but kept off the road. For this experiment all strip roads were brushed out prior to cutting. This usually means that on the roads all reproduction over one foot in height is destroyed.

The different methods of brush disposal for the different plots are given in the paper; they included piling and burning brush in different ways.

Conclusions

Disposal of brush increases the damage done to reproduction during a logging operation.

The original survey showed the average number of trees in the regeneration class to be 420 per acre. Of these 210 survived the operation, but it is pointed out that some of these will die later from sun scald and exposure.

The benefits of slash disposal are given as:
1. Many small trees are released from a fatal covering of slash.
2. More area is opened up for reproduction.
3. Fungi hazards are reduced.

The disadvantages are:
1. A larger area is opened up to direct effects of sun and wind.
2. Additional reproduction is destroyed during slash disposal.

[This paper is a brief summary of an unpublished report, and contains supporting data for only one of the conclusions, namely, that one of the disadvantages of brush disposal is the destruction of additional reproduction.]

6. ASPEN GROVE TYPE (1921 burn), 1949: *V. P. van Vlymen*

Purpose

To study the regeneration and rate of growth on approximately 342 square miles in the Iroquois Falls Concession, which were severely burned in 1921. Most of the area was also burned previously in 1916.

Approximately 23 per cent of the area is now occupied by water, waste land, and residual stands; 43 per cent by aspen stands; 16 per cent by pure alder; and only 18 per cent by young softwood or mixedwood stands.

The remarks given in the paper are based on a study of aerial photographs, supplemented by a reconnaissance and the measurement of 23½-acre plots distributed over the area.

Observations

1. The original wet flats are now covered with dense alder. Where the moss had been destroyed as a result of the fires, there is no coniferous reproduction, but where some moss was retained, black spruce is restocking the area, even in locations without seed trees.

2. On 25 per cent of the aspen area, mainly the dry sites, there is no coniferous regeneration. Throughout the whole aspen area the maximum quantity noted was 35 stems per acre, and the over-all average was 14. This regeneration is mainly white spruce and balsam, 4 to 7 feet in height.

3. It will be a long time (over 100 years) before the aspen area will be restocked with spruce and balsam. The only way to hurry this process would be to cut aspen and plant spruce. This is a costly operation, and experimental plantations established twenty years ago have been only moderately successful.

[The lack of coniferous regeneration on a twice-burned area and the uncertainty of its re-establishment by natural means are supported by other investigators. If the only way to re-establish conifers on such areas is by planting (or seeding), the failure or only moderate success of previous plantations emphasizes the need for further experimental work in planting and seeding.]

BROMPTON PULP AND PAPER COMPANY, LIMITED

IN 1948 a regeneration survey on the Company timber limits at Nipigon was carried out by D. R. Stevens, and a brief report was made. The field method used was similar to that of the Forestry Branch of Canada. The survey was for the purpose of determining present stocking conditions following three types of disturbance: fire alone, logging alone, and logging followed by fire. Owing to the small number of quadrats obtained, no definite conclusions were reached.

GREAT LAKES PAPER COMPANY, LIMITED

REGENERATION surveys were started by the Company in 1945 and have been continued each summer since that time for the purpose of determining the nature and extent of spruce and balsam regeneration on five-year-old cut-over areas.

In carrying out these surveys the line plot system of determining stocking was used, but with some variation in its application. For example, during the 1948 season the quadrat size was changed from 1/600 acre to 1/1000 acre, and four of these quadrats were taken at the end of each chain. During all other seasons, including 1949, the quadrat size of 1/600 acre was used with one quadrat taken at the end of each chain.

In addition to this change, which affected only one season's work, the distance between lines over the years ranged from 4 to 20 chains, depending largely on the size of the tract surveyed, the lines being farther apart on the larger areas.

The reproduction recorded on the quadrats was separated into three size classes:

A—under 6 inches but over 2 inches in height.

B—from 6 inches to 3 feet in height.

C—over 3 feet in height and under 6 inches d.b.h. (breast height measurements recorded in even inches, e.g., one inch d.b.h. includes measurements from 0.6 inches to 1.5 inches.)

For every quadrat a record of each species occurring was kept, this to provide the stocking percentages. On every fifth quadrat a complete tally of all regeneration over two inches in height was taken, this to provide the number per acre figures. In each case individuals were tallied only if they were obviously healthy. In addition, a record was kept for each quadrat of the occurrence of stumps, residual and dead trees by species and diameter classes, this to provide a description of the previous stand.

In some of the surveys layerings were separated from seedlings, but in the later surveys this separation was not attempted.

General descriptive notes of each forest type and cut-over area were made. These included comments on age of the former stand, windfall since cut, number and species of seed trees, dominant herbaceous vegetation and underbrush, drainage, topography, mineral soil, and distribution and mortality of regeneration.

Since an important part of the object of these surveys seems to have been the delimiting of areas unsatisfactorily stocked to pulpwood species, there has been throughout an effort towards the establishment of acceptable stocking standards. Thus two sets of standards are used by this company, one for the upland types and a slightly different one for the swamp types. It is pointed out that, to be fully stocked, the swamps should have 600 well-distributed spruce stems per acre regardless of the balsam content. On the uplands, 600 well-distributed spruce and balsam stems must be present on the acre with a minimum of 200 spruce before that area can be said to be stocked to spruce. If 600 or more balsam only are present the area would be classed as being stocked to balsam only. Certain allowances are made in the interpretation of these rules on areas referred to as marginal, where a total of 600 stems per acre is not present, but where spruce and balsam are well distributed and well mixed with other tree regeneration. The classes now in use are as follows:

	Percentage of 1/600-acre plots stocked		
Fully stocked	90	—	100
Well stocked			
spruce swamps	50	—	89
uplands	60	—	89
Moderately stocked			
spruce swamps	40	—	49
uplands	40	—	59
Poorly stocked	20	—	39
Failure	0	—	19

A brief review of each of the twelve surveys for which reports have been made follows.

1. BLACK STURGEON CONCESSION, 1945: *C. R. Silversides*

Area

The survey was of 9.2 square miles in the Black Sturgeon valley which extends northward from Lake Superior. The area included black spruce swamps 20 per cent; softwoods 2 per cent; mixed softwoods 2 per cent; mixedwoods 47 per cent; hardwoods 29 per cent. It apparently represents part of the forest land cut over in 1936–40, although there is no definite statement indicating exactly what parts of the cut-over area were covered in the survey. Reference is made to Camps 5 and 1.

Results

Fourteen statements are given in the conclusions, five of which are included here.

1. Approximately 85 per cent of the cut-over area is medium stocked or better (medium being 40–70 per cent stocked) and should produce a stand of mature timber equal to that removed.

2. Regeneration on the cut-over land of the same type and same year of cut varied widely.

3. Regeneration appears in the greatest numbers and in the best condition where there is not too much competition from underbrush and ground cover.

4. Advance growth plays a larger role in the regeneration of the upland types than it does in that of the swamps. In the clear cut swamps, with few exceptions, all the residual stand below merchantable size that had been left has died or blown down.

5. Where areas have been cut for saw timber only and the balsam has not been touched, the percentage balsam content of the regeneration shows a marked increase. Areas that have been clear cut for pulpwood or for

pulpwood and saw timber average 30 per cent spruce and 70 per cent balsam regeneration.

[It was not part of the purpose of this survey to explain why regeneration was present or absent. The statements given in the conclusions were meant as information and clues that might be useful in carrying out more intensive investigations. The survey should therefore be looked upon as being in the nature of a trial.]

2. BLACK STURGEON CONCESSION, 1946: *H. Kagetsu*

Area

Stands in the Black Sturgeon Concession, cut over between 1935 and 1941, from the following camps: 1 to 7, 17, 21, and Fog Lake shackers camp.

Results

1. Spruce (with or without balsam) is adequately restocked over 47 per cent of the total area (there are at least 600 softwood stems per acre, including 200 well-distributed spruce). However one-sixth of this area contains a bare minimum of spruce and much balsam.

2. Balsam (without spruce) is adequately restocked over 31 per cent of the total area (at least 600 balsam stems per acre).

3. Brush-covered waste land and other areas of failure comprise 22 per cent of the total.

4. Spruce budworm damage is widespread and serious, though patchy in occurrence. In general both spruce and balsam are attacked, the less vigorous and less healthy trees being most susceptible.

5. In the swamps, spruce regeneration is good, both spruce and balsam beginning to come in during the spring following logging.

6. On the uplands, unless advance growth is present very little spruce comes in. Reasons advanced for this are: (a) competition of broad-leaved shrubs and trees; (b) poor condition of seedbed owing to broad-leaf litter. When spruce seedlings were observed they were usually on rotten logs.

7. Only rarely was slash observed to be effectively harming balsam regeneration. That slash was having a harmful effect on spruce was doubtful.

8. Upland areas of failure invariably contain dense shrub growth. However, advance growth does not appear to suffer from shrubbery.

9. Wet swamps usually have a dense growth of alders with little spruce or balsam regeneration.

10. All of the young aspen, but not the older trees, were observed to be attacked by the poplar leaf miner (*Lithocolletis tremuloidiella*).

11. Areas of failure are most common in the mixedwood type on southern or western aspects where the soil is sandy or silty. Next most common area of failure is found in the black spruce swamp type where excessive changes in the water level have had an adverse effect.

12. The percentage of balsam in the next crop will be greatly increased over that in the last. The mill should consider the possibility of treating balsam as the chief species.

13. Regeneration stocking:

Type	No. of quadrats	Number per acre		Stocking % to	% to
		Spruce	Balsam	spruce	balsam
Black spruce swamp	1319	530	360	50	28
Softwood	818	230	970	21	79
Mixed softwood	652	40	90	42	84
Mixedwood	5329	210	1080	20	68
Hardwood	591	180	800	18	52
All	8709	240	850	26	65

[For purposes of determining stocking the greatest reliance has been placed, in this survey, upon stems per acre as determined from the tally plots (quadrats). In Kagetsu's words: "The percentage of 'occurrence plots' 'successfully restocked' is merely indicative of distribution and far from being mathematically sound. That is to say, if a hypothetical area containing exactly 600 seedlings per acre evenly spaced were to be sampled by the adopted means, it would be impossible to obtain 100% of quadrats 'successfully restocked.' "

J. A. C. Grant's review of this report comments on this statement. "Presumably he means that the 600 trees would not be distributed *exactly* evenly over the acre, hence occasionally a 1/600 acre quadrat would draw a blank. Now if we consider his hypothetical area and allow any tree to deviate 1/5 of the normal spacing, then a blank quadrat will be encountered in 5% of the cases, or in general 25/n% where 1/n is the allowable deviation from the normal spacing. However in practice a considerable portion of the area will be over-stocked with little opportunity of providing 'false blanks.' Hence we can look upon the results of the stocking quadrats as being low by a *maximum* of 5%. Providing the size of quadrat is correctly chosen (a complicated and uncertain matter) stocking quadrat results should be much more reliable than per acre figures taken from tally quadrats."

Kagetsu acknowledges that stocking percentages should be used to determine whether the regeneration is well distributed or not, and presumably some areas with sufficient stems per acre for satisfactory stocking will, because of poor distribution, be classed as unsatisfactory. He does not indicate, however, how stems per acre and per cent of quadrats stocked can be combined in a consistent way to arrive at an intelligible estimate of stocking.

The uncertainty regarding the value of stocking percentages and stocking in numbers per acre in connection with all regeneration surveys has given concern. Until our knowledge of stand development is greatly increased it will be impossible to give exact values to such figures.]

3. Lac des Mille Lacs Concession, 1946: *M. R. McKay*

Area

Stands in the concession, cut over between 1936 and 1939 from **three** camps, known as Ehn's Camp, Camp 102, and Anderson's Camp.

Results

1. Generally over the whole area surveyed, spruce regeneration is good and balsam scarce on the swamp areas.

2. On the uplands, where cutting has been the only disturbance of the original stands, the spruce regeneration is fair only, and that of balsam is good.

3. On the uplands most of the seedlings have come in since the cut; this is apparent from the fact that they occur most profusely where the stand has been more completely opened up.

4. In the burned area of the upland cutover very few seedlings of either spruce or balsam are present.

5. Seed trees are very scattered in parts of the swamp cutover, yet regeneration appears adequate. Distances up to fifteen chains from seed trees have been seeded. In the uplands seed trees are much more plentiful.

6. After seven to ten years, slash does not appear to be a serious obstacle to present seeding or seedling growth either in swamps or in uplands.

Conclusions

1. As a whole, the cut-over areas surveyed are restocking satisfactorily.

2. The upland area, however, now has a much larger percentage of balsam than that in the former stand. Most of the spruce should remain under ordinary conditions, whereas the thickly clumped balsam will thin itself out and the high ratio of balsam to spruce will be reduced.

3. Spruce regeneration predominates in the swamps. All of it has appeared since the cut.

4. The method of survey used gives a very small sample of the area, and the figures quoted cannot be accepted with accuracy.

[The reason given in support of the finding that most of the seedlings on the uplands have come in since the cut (see (3) under "Results") is not acceptable. Places where the stand had been completely opened up might well be the parts of the original stand where the greatest amount of advance reproduction occurred. Nowhere in the report is there evidence that seeding-in of the cutover is taking place, or that the seedlings tallied are reproduction since logging, or that they are advance growth. It is also difficult to agree with the last part of conclusion (3), which states that all of the spruce in the swamps has appeared since the cut. It would be a very unusual uncut spruce swamp that did not have within it some layerings or spruce seedlings.]

4. LAC DES MILLE LACS CONCESSION, 1947: *M. R. McKay*

Area

Joynt and Savanne townships, about 75 miles west of Fort William on the C.P.R. and the Trans-Canada Highway. The survey was confined to the areas around Camps 100 and 102 on swamp sites (intermediate between wooded muskeg and uplands). The terrain is quite flat with poor to fair drainage. The forest had been clear cut for spruce and balsam to a minimum top diameter of 4 inches in 1941–2, and to some extent previous to that, and was about 135 years old.

Results

The general conclusions stated in the report are that spruce regeneration is good and balsam sparse. At Camp 100 there are a number of small areas of failure up to 3 acres in size. Camp 102 has two areas of failure totalling 22.5 acres. Failure in these areas is evidently caused by poor drainage, heavy alder and grass growth, and the poor condition of the seedbed. Spruce and balsam regeneration beneath alders will probably not survive.

A summary of the recorded data taken from pages 4 and 5 in the report is given in Table XXII.

[The last column of Table XXII is somewhat misleading, the figures revealing an almost perfect condition. A more useful and realistic picture is obtained from the percentages given in the last column under "Stocking Quadrats."]

5. ENGLISH RIVER CONCESSION, 1947: *W. M. Henderson*

Area

Camps 300, 301, and 302 situated north of Wintering Lake, and southwest of Valora on the branch line of the C.N.R. between Fort William and Superior Junction. The area was cut over for pulpwood in 1942–3.

The terrain is flat with very gently rolling uplands and flat low-lying swamps. Drainage is generally good in the former and fair in the latter.

Results

1. No areas of failure exist.

2. The swamps are satisfactorily stocked with spruce and should produce a crop equal to that removed.

3. On the uplands spruce is very sparse, but balsam is plentiful, being very dense on half the area. Poplar is the dominant tree.

4. The area north of, and within two or three miles of, Wintering Lake appears to have an abnormally high proportion of balsam, both in the old crop and in the regeneration.

5. In the swamps, most of the balsam was established before the cut, and at least 75 per cent of the spruce after the cut.

6. On the uplands, probably 95 per cent of the balsam was established before the cut.

7. Although there is some evidence that slash is holding back regeneration, its effect is relatively insignificant.

The data given below in Table XXIII represent a summary of the recorded data, taken from Tables 1–5 in the report.

TABLE XXII

SUMMARY OF RECORDED DATA, LAC DES MILLES LACS CONCESSION, 1947

Camp	Cut per acre (cords)	% Balsam	Drainage	Stocking quadrats					List quadrats						
				No. of quadrats	% Sampled	Spruce %	Balsam %	Either %	No. of quadrats	% Sampled	Spruce per acre	Balsam per acre	Total per acre	Balsam %	% Area stocking satisfactory
100	20.6	0.4	poor	626	0.11	61	14	68	121	0.02	1260	140	1400	10	100
102	17.6	1.7	fair	303	0.18	55	10	69	59	0.04	1340	100	1440	7	92
Both				929		62	13	68	180		1290	130	1420	9	98

TABLE XXIII

SUMMARY OF RECORDED DATA, ENGLISH RIVER CONCESSION, 1947

Camp and site	Cut per acre (cords)	% Balsam	Stocking quedrats					List quadrats					
			No. of quadrats	% Sampled	Spruce %	Balsam %	Either %	No. of quadrats	% Sampled	Spruce per acre	Balsam per acre	Total per acre	% Balsam
300	13.5	30		.09					02				
BSS-2			111		68	44	87	22		1391	1555	2946	53
M			170		19	89	89	31		176	6058	6232	97
S			66		15	76	77	12		600	2650	3250	82
301	16.5	13		.10					02				
BSS-2			72		64	35	75	14		2700	900	3600	25
M			75		20	87	87	15		360	4920	5280	93
S			37		46	64	92	7		1714	1800	3514	51
S-1			16		31	69	75	3		4000	3000	7000	43
302	14.7	1		.14					03				
BSS-2			158		61	9	68	29		1095	0	1095	0
ALL					42	55	81						

BSS-2—Black spruce swamp; S—Softwood; S-1—Immature softwood; M—Mixedwood.

6. BLACK STURGEON CONCESSION, 1948: *C. F. Phinney*

Area

Forest cut over during the 1942–3 season from Camps 4A, 6, 7, 8, 9, 10, and 16, and the area cut in 1941–2 at Camp 2. Field work was completed in approximately two months.

Results

Areas of failure are given for each camp. Seedling location is discussed for spruce and balsam in the swamps and on the uplands, and with reference to this the following observations are made:

1. A great percentage of the regeneration established on upland areas, especially spruce, is of an age which confirms its existence prior to the years of the cutting operations [no supporting data].

2. The swamp type differs from the uplands in that almost 100 per cent of the seedlings appear to have been established since the cut was made.

There is a short discussion on seed trees in the swamps and on the uplands with the observation, among others, that spruce and balsam regeneration was found to be consistently better within short distances of existing stands.

The final pages of the report deal with the following items: topography, surface soil, sub-soil, site, drainage, humus, ground cover, underbrush, soil exposure, seedbed conditions, slope and aspect, amount and decay of slash, effects of slash, effects on conifer regeneration by hardwood regeneration and by ground cover and underbrush, residual stand, regeneration mortality, the sampling system (with suggested changes), field procedure, and a one-page general summation.

[The report is poorly put together with the data presented by camps (eight in number) so that there are pages of tables which tend to confuse rather than assist the reader. The total number of quadrats taken on each area is shown but these quadrats are not broken down by forest cover types. This can be done with a small amount of work and reference to the maps and to the areas of forest types cut over, but such additional work is troublesome to any reader.

It is but fair to add here that the author of the report was at the time an undergraduate forestry student and that he conducted two different regeneration surveys in the one season.]

7. ENGLISH RIVER CONCESSION, 1948: *C. F. Phinney*

Area

Forest cut over during the 1943–4 season from Camps 300, 301, 302, 303, and 304. Field work was completed in 10 days.

Results

The following observations are taken from the general summation at the end of the report.

1. All upland areas are generally well stocked with balsam, while spruce

is comparatively very scarce. A large percentage of the spruce present was established prior to the cutting operation.

2. The swamps are very poorly restocked with spruce, and it is doubtful if this condition will improve until the slash has decayed enough to allow seedling establishment.

3. No areas of complete failure were found although some swamps are so poorly stocked that they have the general appearance of failure.

4. Underbrush and slash appear to be the greatest obstacles to better restocking of spruce in the swamps.

5. From observations made and the samples examined, it appears that the former swamp stand will not be replaced by a stand of similar density unless there is an improvement in the present conditions.

[The report is on the same plan as that written for the Black Sturgeon Concession by the same writer, and has the same weaknesses as were pointed out for that report.]

8. BLACK STURGEON CONCESSION, 1949: *R. L. Abbott*

Area

Forest cut over during the 1943–4 season at Camps 3, 6, 7, 9, 11, 12, and 16 on the Black Sturgeon Concession some 50 miles northeast of Fort William.

Results

1. Tally results, taken from the summary table for the Black Sturgeon Limit in the report, are shown in Table XXIV.

TABLE XXIV

TALLY OF REGENERATION, BLACK STURGEON CONCESSION, 1949

Type	Number of quadrats	Percentage of quadrats stocked				
		Spruce	Balsam	Spr. and Bal.	Spr. or Bal.	Unstocked
BSS	648	44.7	31.2	15.9	60.0	37.1
S	352	24.2	69.6	21.0	79.5	26.4
MS	712	25.6	55.0	12.8	68.0	32.4
M	805	26.2	65.0	19.0	72.0	27.6

Type	Number of quadrats	Stems per acre					
		Spruce	Balsam	Poplar	Birch	Tamarack	Jack pine
BSS	125	1160	670	120		5	
S	65	400	2550	175	110		
MS	131	350	1680	395	10	10	85
M	157	530	1610	100	40		

BSS—Black spruce swamp; S—Softwood; MS—Mixed softwood; M—Mixedwood.

2. In the swamps spruce stocking is recorded as moderate (40–9 per cent); one small area is well stocked (50–89 per cent). Balsam stocking is moderate.

On the uplands spruce stocking is recorded as very poor to failure (0–39 per cent) with balsam well stocked (60–89 per cent).

3. 5.65 per cent of the total area is classed as failure.

4. Conifer regeneration was not observed to increase under or near residual stands or near scattered residuals in either swamp or upland.

[The inclusion of the basis plots (quadrats) in the various tables given and the addition of a summary table greatly increases the value of this report over the 1948 ones. The main weakness lies in the presentation of the material.]

9. ENGLISH RIVER CONCESSION, 1949: *G. W. Cameron*

Area

The forest area cut over in 1944–5 from Camps 300, 301, 303, and 304.

It is stated that, during the period under study, some 2230 acres were cut over from these camps. Obviously the cutting was in 1944–5 and not at the time of the regeneration study (see summary below).

Results

The data are presented for each camp. They show that the swamps are generally well stocked or moderately stocked to spruce at all four locations. The uplands are generally well stocked to balsam, but are poorly stocked to spruce at two camps and moderately stocked to spruce at the other two. At two camps small areas were classed as being inadequately stocked to conifer regeneration.

Table XXV gives the information about stocking obtained.

In the last part of the report the types are described and some of the factors influencing the regeneration of spruce and balsam are referred to. It is suggested that no single factor is responsible for lack of conifer reproduction and that the factors favouring spruce reproduction are not similar to those favouring balsam.

[The results obtained at Camps 300 and 301 in this survey and in the 1947 survey (see No. 5 in this section) indicate that the stocking of spruce reproduction on the cut-over areas examined ranges from 19 to 76 per cent, being high in the swamp types and low on the uplands. The range in the different types is as follows: in the BSS (swamp) 64 to 76 per cent, in the S (softwood) 15 to 29, and in the M (mixedwood) 19 to 24 per cent. On the other hand, the stocking of balsam reproduction ranges from 29 to 89 per cent and is highest on the uplands. Its range in the different types is: BSS 29 to 44, S 56 to 83, and M 78 to 89.

These percentages agree closely with the findings of investigators elsewhere in the Province.]

TABLE XXV
STOCKING, ENGLISH RIVER CONCESSION, 1949

Year of cut: 1944–5
Area cut over by types:

BSS	565 acres
S	586 acres
M	1081 acres

Total area cut over: 2232 acres
Percentage of cruise: 0.15
Total number of sample quadrats: 1969
Size of quadrat: 1/600 acre
Total length of strips run: 24.6 miles
Total area of failure by types:

BSS	29.4 acres
S	32.9 acres
M	11.5 acres

73.8 acres
Percentage of failure: 3.3

Percentage of Quadrats Stocked

Type	Number of quadrats	Spruce	Balsam	Sp. and Bal.	Sp. or Bal.	Unstocked to spruce or balsam
BSS	379	68	33	22	79	21
S	480	33	69	22	80	20
M	990	24	77	18	83	17
	1849					

Seedlings per Acre
(Based on fifth quadrat tally)

Type	Number of quadrats	Spruce	Balsam	Poplar	Birch
BSS	73	1520	570	30	
S	90	430	2270	410	30
M	189	410	2170	680	30
	352				

BSS—Black spruce swamp; S—Softwood; M—Mixedwood.

10. LAC DES MILLES LACS CONCESSION, 1949: *G. W. Cameron*

The field work on which this report is based was done at five different camps, and the data for each camp are presented separately. A summary table covering four of these camps is included. At the four main camp locations the swamps are well stocked to vigorous spruce seedlings. The uplands, however, show wide variation in the regeneration. In the case of spruce, one camp area is classed as a failure, a second as poor, a third as moderately stocked, and the fourth as well stocked. In the case of balsam, three of the camp areas are well stocked, and cne is classed as poorly stocked. The fifth camp area includes only the swamp type, which is given as being moderately stocked to spruce.

The summary table for the area taken from the report is given as Table XXVI.

TABLE XXVI

STOCKING, LAC DES MILLES LACS CONCESSION, 1949

Year of cut: 1943–4
Area cut over by types:

BSS 1367 acres
S   518 acres
M   22 acres

Total area cut over: 1907 acres
Total number of sample quadrats: 1641
Size of quadrat: 1/600 acre
Total area of sample: 2.73 acres
Total length of strips run 20.5 miles
Percentage of cruise: 0.14
Total area of failure: 12 acres
Percentage of failure: 0.63

Percentage of Quadrats Stocked

Type	Number of quadrats	Spruce	Balsam	Sp. and Bal.	Sp. or Bal.	Unstocked
BSS	1220	75	18	13	80	20
S	401	34	75	24	85	16
M*	20	0	65	0	65	35

Stems per Acre
(Based on fifth quadrat tally)

Type	Number of quadrats	Spruce	Balsam	Poplar	Birch
BSS	227	2000	290	5	2
S	75	650	2400	140	65
M*	4		1170	2500	

*Insufficient sampling.

The report also includes a brief description of the types, and a discussion of the factors responsible for regeneration which is not unlike that included in the English River Concession report (No. 9 in this section). The influence of drainage is referred to as being one of the main factors influencing the composition of the regeneration. For example, in the swamps the best spruce regeneration from the standpoint of both occurrence and vigour, was found on the moderately well drained sites rather than on the very wet or very dry sites. In the softwood type a prolific growth of evenly distributed balsam occurred on the drier sites while spruce regeneration was confined to the wetter flats. This statement refers in particular to the regeneration established following the cut.

11. GULL LAKE LIMIT, 1949: G. W. Cameron

The 1943–4 cut-over areas at two company camps about 120 miles northwest of Fort William in the Kenora district were sampled for the data on which this report is based.

At both camps the swamps are reported as being well stocked to spruce. Some variation occurs in the stocking of both spruce and balsam on the uplands. The softwood type was moderately stocked to spruce at both camps, but balsam stocking was poor at one camp and classed as well stocked at the other. In the mixedwood type spruce stocking was poor at both camps, with balsam stocking good.

The summary table for the two areas taken from the report is given in Table XXVII.

The remainder of the report includes a brief description of the types with observations on the factors influencing regeneration.

TABLE XXVII

STOCKING, GULL LAKE LIMIT, 1949

Year of cut: 1943–4
Area cut over: 511 acres
Total number of sample quadrats: 1059
Total area of sample: 1.76 acres
Percentage of cruise: 0.35
Total area of failure: 32.5 acres
Percentage of failure: 6.5

Percentage of Quadrats Stocked

Type	Number of quadrats	Spruce	Balsam	Sp. and Bal.	Sp. or Bal.	Unstocked to spruce or balsam
BSS	649	68	19	13	75	25
S	114	49	65	30	85	15
MS	105	54	29	18	67	33
M	103	19	79	15	85	15
	971					

Seedlings per Acre
(Based on fifth quadrat tally)

Type	Number of quadrats	Spruce	Balsam	Poplar	W. pine
BSS	119	1370	290	30	30
S	22	1000	1000	389	110
MS	20	1200	515	15	
M	20	850	2540	330	
	181				

12. KASHABOWIE LIMIT, 1949: G. W. Cameron

The 1943–4 cut-over areas at two camps were sampled as a basis for this report.

At both camps the swamps are reported as being well stocked to vigorous spruce seedlings. The upland sites at one camp were moderately stocked to both spruce and balsam seedlings, while at the other camp (113) both spruce and balsam stocking was poor.

The summary table for the area taken from the report is given in Table XXVIII.

TABLE XXVIII

STOCKING, KASHABOWIE LIMIT, 1949

Year of cut: 1943–4
Total area of cut: 290 acres
Total number of sample quadrats: 544
Total area of sample: 0.923 acres
Percentage of cruise: 0.31
Total area of failure: 0 acres
Percentage of failure: 0

Percentage of Quadrats Stocked

Type	Number of quadrats	Spruce	Balsam	Sp. and Bal.	Sp. or Bal.	Unstocked to spruce or balsam
BSS	471	62	26	18	70	30
MS	83	41	28	14	55	44
	554					

Seedlings per Acre
(Based on fifth quadrat tally)

Type	Number of quadrats	Spruce	Balsam	Birch	Tamarack	Poplar
BSS	86	1780	400	110	50	
MS	16	680	520	200		320
	102					

The report concludes with a brief description of the types and some observations on the factors influencing regeneration. Regarding the latter, it is pointed out that for the upland areas too little data were collected on which to base definite conclusions.

[The last three reports (Nos. 10, 11, and 12) show that most of the quadrats taken in the surveys were in the BSS type. For all three surveys there were 2340 quadrats in that type with only 826 in the other three together (S, M, and MS). It is not surprising then that the results show relatively high spruce stocking.]

THE KVP COMPANY, LIMITED

EXPERIMENTAL work for the purpose of studying the reproduction of jack pine following logging began in 1948. An interim report on this project was issued in 1949, but at that date too little time had elapsed to enable any conclusions to be drawn. The Forestry Branch, Canada, is co-operating with the Company in the project and will assist in the compilation and analysis of the findings.

The study is being carried out on six demonstration areas, each 2½ acres in area and square, in what was, before cutting, a pure even-aged merchantable jack pine stand that had little or no understory or advance growth. These areas are together known as the Ramsey Demonstration Area. The report includes a detailed description of such matters as location, topography and drainage, soil conditions, vegetation and timber stand for each of the areas before cutting and the following outline of treatments subsequently given to each:

Area I: cut in strips with slash left in windrows, broadcast burned in spring, eastern half (E½) seeded.

Area II: cut in strips with slash lopped and scattered, broadcast burned in spring, E½ seeded.

Area III (control plot): cut in strips with slash left in windrows, S½ seeded.

Area IV: cut in strips, scarified with Athens plow and slash lopped and scattered, S½ seeded.

Area V: cable skidded in tree lengths, slash lopped and scattered on S½ only.

Area VI: cut and bunched and then tractor skidded, slash lopped and scattered on S½ only.

[These differently treated areas were visited by the reviewer in August, 1949, and it was noted that on many of the bared places within them seedlings of jack pine were coming in, but that where the soil was covered with undisturbed litter there were no seedlings.]

LONGLAC PULP AND PAPER COMPANY, LIMITED

FOREST regeneration studies by this Company began about 1946 and two reports have been issued, one of which, being mainly concerned with the limits of the Spruce Falls Power and Paper Company, is reviewed under that section (see p. 133). The method used in conducting the survey reviewed here was the same as that used by the Spruce Falls Power and Paper Company except for a few minor variations in classifying the sites.

There is some indication that spruce regeneration on some of the cut-over areas is somewhat better than that reported in the surveys of the Kapuskasing area (see pp. 130–4). There are, however, insufficient records available to enable any definite statement. In the report reviewed here the data reveal, for the majority of the sites, a condition of the forest regeneration that is very similar to that on the Spruce Falls Power and Paper Company limits and not unlike that reported by other investigators elsewhere in the Province. The II-B type (spruce flat) is the one exception. It shows the highest percentage of spruce, approximately double that on the slopes.

REGENERATION SURVEY, 1949: *E. R. Sexsmith*

Purpose

To determine the distribution of the coniferous regeneration on the older cut-over areas.

Method

Line plot system; lines 3 to 10 chains apart crossing the strip roads at an angle. Quadrats of 1/600 acre were taken at the end of each chain. Spruce, balsam, and jack pine were tallied for stocking and a complete count of all species was made on every 10th quadrat.

Three main sites were recognized: slopes, flats, and muskeg. The first two of these are subdivided mainly on the basis of species.

Site I: Well-drained land over which surplus water runoff is good. Scant moss cover and thin humus layer (1"–3"). Hardwood is usually present.

I-S: Pure conifer. Original stand was more than 75 per cent softwood and less than 50 per cent of the softwood was jackpine.

I-Pj: Pure conifer. Original stand was more than 75 per cent softwood and more than 50 per cent of the softwood was jackpine.

I-M: Mixed. Original stand between 75 and 25 per cent conifer.

I-H: Hardwood. Original stand less than 25 per cent conifer.

Site II: Draina e is not free running and water is evident for some time after heavy precipitation. The water table is not high enough to stunt growth. Humus layer generally over 6" thick.

II-A: Spruce, balsam, and birch were left after cutting. Balsam residuals pedominate; 1-inch and 2-inch trees are common. Labrador tea and sphagnum are usually absent. This is almost a transitional type between sites I and II but the soil is definitely site II rather than site I.

II-B: Spruce flat, with very little balsam. Labrador tea in abundance, considerable residual stand of spruce and often much alder, both young and old (originating before or since the cut).

II-C: Spruce flat, clean cut. Originally a good stand; stumps plentiful. Practically no advance growth. Labrador tea and sphagnum common and new alders may or may not be present.

II-D: Spruce tamarack swamp, often with cedar, old alders, and considerable residual stand. Sphagnum fairly common but labrador tea much less in evidence. The area has been only lightly cut over. Good leader growth.

Site III: Merchantable muskeg. Drainage poor with water table close to surface. Diameter and height growth retarded. Humus layer thick, often measuring several feet. Stunted spruce left in abundance. Stumps are few and small. Sphagnum moss in hummocks. Labrador tea and its associates often form a complete cover. Few alders.

The main results of the survey are given in Table XXIX.

TABLE XXIX

STOCKING PERCENTAGES FOR SPRUCE AND BALSAM BY YEARS AND
SITE TYPES, LONGLAC PULP AND PAPER COMPANY LIMITS*

Type	1938 cut	'39	'40	'41	'42	'43	'44	'45
				Spruce				
I–S	25	49	43	50	34		29	27
I–M	27	31	29	32	25		16	
I–Pj					4	20		
II–A	27	32	35	28	28		19	
II–B	54	53	48	38	44		26	
II–D	45		23	22				
				Balsam				
I–S	41	57	42	41	36		26	4
I–M	67	76	63	75	68		56	
I–Pj					2	1		
II–A	63	70	53	56	57		27	
II–B	22	39	36	34	36		28	
II–D	35		37	47				
Number of quadrats	1119	945	2236	2764	1755	220	1246	151

*All percentages based on a very low quadrat number have been omitted.

Spruce regeneration seldom shows more than 50 per cent stocking with the highest degrees of stocking in the older cutovers. The poorest stocking occurs in the I-M type and the best in the II-B type.

In the case of balsam the best stocking occurs in the I-M type with the poorest in the wetter II types.

In conclusion the writer states that, unless balsam regeneration will satisfy mill requirements, steps should be taken to increase the proportion of spruce, especially in the I-M type.

MARATHON PAPER MILLS OF CANADA, LIMITED

THIS company has been carrying out forest regeneration surveys since 1948, and, in co-operation with the Department of Lands and Forests, surveys and experiments of various kinds have also been undertaken. The surveys carried out in co-operation with the Department of Lands and Forests are reviewed in the section assigned to the Department (see No. 18).

One report for the company was made in 1949, *Regeneration Surveys on Mechanically Operated Areas*, by W. D. Harkness. This gives a summary of the results of regeneration surveys carried out at Camp 2, Stevens district, during 1948 and 1949, but at the present time it is felt that these surveys, representing as they do a rather limited sample, may not be indicative of the forest conditions.

From the various studies that have been made, however, the following conclusions with regard to the problem of forest regeneration have been reached.

1. Arbitrary stocking standards are not particularly suitable for determining good or poor stocking, and may even be misleading.

For example, in the Pic area, to all intents and purposes a virgin forest, the stands now existing in mature age classes may justifiably be considered fully stocked for any specific site condition. The aim should therefore be to get on this area, when it is cut, a stocking equivalent to the present one, or if possible, by management, to improve on it.

The following table shows the productivity of these mature stands and the existing stems per acre:

Cover type	Cords per acre	Stems per acre
Conifer	30.9	264
Softwood	28.7	267
Mixedwood	42.2	044
Hardwood	42.0	237

This table should indicate the required stocking. The degree of stocking for the next crop should therefore be determined on the basis of the existing stems per acre.

2. Distribution of stocking is as important as degree of stocking. A volume per acre equal to that indicated above and assumed to be normal for the Pic area can only be obtained if the present available growing space is fully used.

3. Practically all regeneration surveys emphasize the importance of spruce and balsam. The Pic area classification of cover type is as follows:

Conifer	33.0%
Swamp spruce	18.5%
Upland spruce	13.1%
Jack pine	1.5%

Softwood   8.1%
Mixedwood   52.2%
Hardwood   3.7%

It is apparent from the above that the regeneration of poplar, birch, and other species should also be considered, as they form the largest part of the growing stock in the Pic area. Instead of being discarded, either fully or partially, these should be considered and the mill and logging processes prepared for full utilization of all species. This is being done by the Company.

4. Regeneration in the Pic area is not in itself a problem. The objective is not so much a matter of suitable stocking as it is the shortening of the regeneration period by modification of logging techniques and by forest protection.

[The first of these conclusions emphasizes again the prevailing dissatisfaction with regard to standards of stocking. The number of stems at present in a mature stand does not, however, reveal the percentage of stocking in the stand at 5, 10, 15 or n years of age, and therefore cannot be used as a standard. It may well indicate what we want to get at some future date. The real question, then, is, what stocking is necessary at present to get that number in the future. Standards of stocking as set up by different individuals are not intended to do more than indicate present conditions. If an area is only half stocked at present for any one species, it is assumed that it will remain that way unless seeding-in of the particular species is taking place.

Regarding conclusion (3), it may be said that the difficulties encountered in getting spruce regeneration are the main reasons for the emphasis placed on that species. In the problem of forest regeneration all commercial species are important, but those that are of high use value yet reproduce with difficulty should undoubtedly receive first attention.]

NEWAYGO TIMBER COMPANY, LIMITED

ONE survey has been made, representing the first step towards assessing the value of the reproduction on the company timber limits.

The method of carrying out this survey differs from that of all others and it is therefore difficult to compare the results obtained with those of other surveys. Moreover the number of quadrats on which the percentages are based is not given in the report.

The main features of the report are given below.

TEMPLETON TOWNSHIP, ALGOMA DISTRICT, 1948: *H. O. Kantola*

Purpose

To determine whether good and poor seed years had any effect on regeneration while cutting was in progress and to estimate the possibility of reproducing a stand equal to that cut during 1926–42.

Method

Line plot system. Plots, consisting of 20 quadrats (1/1000 acre in size) were placed at ten-chain intervals on a line. The quadrats in each plot were taken in groups of 4, the groups being one chain apart so that the plot extended over a distance of 4¾ chains. All tree species were tallied as either regeneration or advance growth, the former being seedlings established subsequent to the disturbance and the latter being seedlings established before the disturbance. Stocking standards were established, using the group of 4 mil-acre quadrats as one unit, as follows:

Fully stocked: at least one good seedling on each of the four quadrats.

Good stocking: at least one good seedling on each of three of the four quadrats.

Fair stocking: at least one good seedling on each of two of the four quadrats.

Poor stocking: at least one good seedling on one of the four quadrats.

Failure: all four quadrats without seedlings.

Residual trees, stumps, and site conditions were recorded. Twenty-four miles of line were run, giving a total of 780 quadrats on an area of cutover of a little over 6,000 acres.

Observations

Of the area cut over in 1926–31, 62 per cent is adequately stocked, 32 per cent partially stocked, and 6 per cent a complete failure.

Of the area cut over in 1934–42, 34 per cent is adequately stocked, 33 per cent partially stocked, and 22 per cent a failure.

Supporting tables are given for these percentages.

There was no evidence that the regeneration was any better in any particular year, indicating no correlation between seed year and cut.

123

ONTARIO-MINNESOTA PULP AND PAPER COMPANY, LIMITED

REPRODUCTION surveys were carried out by the Company in 1946 and in 1950. A summary of the results for each season has been kept and a report was made of the 1950 survey. In 1946 the line plot system of survey was used, with quadrats 1/600 acre in size at intervals of 50 feet on the strip. Lines or strips were at 400-foot intervals. In 1950 the quadrat size was changed to 1/1000 acre to make the figures obtained comparable to those of the Department of Lands and Forests, and the lines were spaced 1000 feet apart instead of 400. On each quadrat the presence of seedlings and advance growth of all species not exceeding 4.5 inches d.b.h. was noted. On every 10th quadrat the exact number of each species present was recorded by size classes:

> 0–0.5 feet
> 0.5′–0.5″ d.b.h.
> 0.5″ d.b.h.–2.5″ d.b.h.
> 2.5″ d.b.h.–4.5″ d.b.h.
> over 4.5″ d.b.h.

Cotyledonous seedlings were not tallied.

Notes were made to enable classification of the recorded data. In these notes were described:

1. Any disturbance such as cut, burn, cut and burn, burn and cut, infestation, and the number of years since it took place.

2. The original type.

3. Topography and moisture, using such terms as: S, swamp, poorly drained; L, lowland, better drained but with high water table; US, upland slope, well drained; U, upland, well-drained level ground, ridge; etc.

4. Depth of soil and type.

5. Density of herbaceous vegetation.

6. Crown canopy.

7. Whether the quadrat occurred on a road or the strip between roads.

8. Number of spruce and balsam seed trees within a radius of 66 feet of the quadrat which are healthy enough to have borne seeds.

Tables XXX and XXXI, taken from data supplied by the Company, summarize some of the results obtained to 1950.

[The results shown in the tables although admittedly inadequate to be conclusive, are not unlike those obtained for similar types by other investigators using quadrats of 1/600 acre size.]

TABLE XXX

PERCENT STOCKING BY YEARS AFTER CUTTING, SEINE RIVER CONCESSION, 1946

Type	After 5–10 years (Based on 6808 quadrats)				After 15 to 20 years (Based on 2595 quadrats)			
	Spr.	*Bal.*	*J.pine*	*W.pine*	*Spr.*	*Bal.*	*J.pine*	*W.pine*
Black spruce	53	7	2		64	14	3	4
Spruce–balsam	37	75		3	44	75		
Jack pine	38	5	6		50	5	5	4
Mixedwood	28	25	1	1	25	57	3	6

TABLE XXXI

PERCENT STOCKING 5–10 YEARS AFTER CUTTING, LAKE OF THE WOODS CONCESSION (NESTOR)
(Based on 741 quadrats)

Type	Spruce	Balsam	Jack pine	Poplar	Birch	Other hwds.	Cedar	Tamarack
Black spruce	37	21		17	4	1	6	4
Spruce–balsam	14	52			5		5	5
Jack pine	13	25	13	38				
Mixedwood	4	12		66	6			
Hardwood	3	12		64	4	1		

THE SPRUCE FALLS POWER AND PAPER COMPANY, LIMITED

REGENERATION surveys on cut-over areas have formed a part of the woods work of the Company since 1933. In the first surveys regeneration was recorded in numbers per acre, a method which gave an incomplete, and even misleading, picture of the actual conditions. This fact was realized early in the survey work and the system of recording data was altered to include the use of the stocked quadrat. By making use of two kinds of plots, one known as the list quadrat and the other as the stocked quadrat, it was possible to determine not only the number of individuals per acre but also to indicate their distribution or frequency of occurrence.

This was such an important change in survey methods that the essential features of the system that developed have been adopted by all others conducting regeneration surveys in the Province.

The main features of the method are as follows. A quadrat of 1/600 acre in size is taken at the end of each chain on compass lines which are up to 10 chains apart. All quadrats are tallied on a stocking record sheet and in addition every 10th quadrat is tallied on a stand sheet. On the stocking record sheets is recorded only the presence or absence of the species on all used quatrats. On the stand sheet is recorded a complete count of all the species occurring on every tenth quadrat. The stocking record sheets give the frequency of occurrence (distribution) for each species. The stand sheets give the number per acre of each species. (A complete description is given in the Appendix to Part I.)

The surveys conducted by the Company indicate that some of the cut-over areas, mainly on the well-drained sites, are not reproducing satisfactorily and experiments that have been carried out have not indicated any way of obtaining natural reproduction of spruce on these sites.

For the convenience of the reader a short description of the cover types used in these surveys is included.

Site I: Well-drained land over which surplus water runoff is good. This type is characterized by a scant moss cover and thin humus layer. Hardwoods are usually present in the composition of the stands, although pure stands of conifer occur.

I—P: Pure conifer. Original stand more than 80 per cent conifer.

I—M: Mixed. Original stand less than 80 per cent conifer.

Site II: Areas over which the drainage is not free running and water is evident for some time after heavy precipitation. The water table is not high enough to stunt growth. The humus layer is thick, generally over six inches.

II—A: Spruce, balsam, and birch present amongst the residuals. Balsam residuals predominate; 1-inch and 2-inch trees are common. Labrador tea and sphagnum moss are usually absent.

II—B: Spruce flat, with very little balsam. There is a considerable residual stand and often much alder both young and old (originating before or since the cut). Labrador tea is present in abundance.

II—C: Spruce flat, clean cut. Originally a good stand; the stumps are large and plentiful. There is practically no advance growth. Labrador tea and sphagnum moss are common, and alders that come in following cutting may or may not be present.

II—D: Spruce–tamarack swamp, often with cedar. Alders of the previous stand are often found with a considerable residual tree stand. Sphagnum moss is fairly common with labrador tea much less in evidence. The original stand was poor and has been only lightly cut over. The type is not a muskeg, as there are excellent leaders on the residual spruce trees.

Site III: Merchantable muskeg. Drainage is poor with the water table reaching close to the surface through the sphagnum moss. Diameter and height growth are retarded. The humus layer is thick, often measuring several feet. Stunted spruce, left after cutting, are abundant. The cut was poor, and stumps are few and small. Sphagnum moss appears in hummocks, and labrador tea and its associates often form a complete cover. There are few, if any, alders.

1. REGENERATION STUDIES, 1933: *J. B. Millar*

Purpose

To determine the quantity of reproduction on the 1928–9 cutover from Camp 3.

Method

A continuous 3-foot wide strip on which the seedlings were counted.

Observations

1. No seedlings were found on the main haul roads and tote roads where there is grass.

2. No seedlings were found under slash.

3. Where labrador tea is abundant spruce regeneration is confined to openings.

4. On one site (II—C) practically all the new spruce seedlings are on clumps of sphagnum moss.

5. On the area burned in 1929 no seedlings were found except on isolated patches of sphagnum moss.

6. Balsam seedlings occur under more cover than do spruce and under deeper slash.

7. In general, the advance growth has completely recovered from suppression.

Table XXXII, taken from the report, gives the essential data.

2. REGENERATION STUDIES, 1938: *E. Bonner*

During the period 1933 to 1938 a regeneration survey was made each

TABLE XXXII

REGENERATION IN NUMBERS PER ACRE ON A CUT-OVER AREA,
KAPUSKASING DISTRICT, 1933

Site	Location	Spruce	Balsam	Spruce percentage of total seedlings
1 Pure	Strip*	941	20,754	4.3
1-P	Road	1749	20,079	8.0
1 Mixed	Strip	1559	31,837	4.7
1-M	Road	4800	18,000	21.1
II-A	Strip	1057	15,264	6.5
II-A	Road	2548	16,359	13.5
II-B	Strip	2060	8615	19.3
II-B	Road	4846	16,897	22.3
II-C	Strip	1473	2527	36.8
II-C	Road	6214	2762	69.2
II-D	Strip	2513	4479	35.9
II-D	Road	3432	5270	39.4
III-C	Strip	778	1333	36.9
III-C	Road	4000	2000	66.7
	TOTAL	37,970	166,176	384.6
	AVERAGE	2712	11,870	27.5

*Strip—The area between the access roads that is generally covered with slash.

year on a portion of cut-over land and a report was prepared at the end of each season's work. The results of these surveys have been included in a combined table in this 1938 report, thus making unnecessary the inclusion of a review of the 1934, 1935, 1936, and 1937 reports.

The purpose of the 1938 survey was essentially the same as for the previous ones: to determine the quantity and distribution of spruce and balsam regeneration on cut-over areas. The survey was in the 1932–3 cutover from Camp 12.

The stocked quadrat method as developed during the previous four surveys was used.

Observations

1. Stocking for spruce was slightly higher than the previous average, probably because 1932 was a good seed year for spruce. There was no noticeable change in balsam stocking.

2. On all sites there was a high percentage of blanks owing to heavy slash piles.

3. On Site II the best seedbed for spruce is the compact hummocks of the small-headed type of sphagnum moss.

Table XXXIII, taken from the report, shows the main results.

TABLE XXXIII

PERCENTAGE OF 1/600 ACRE QUADRATS STOCKED TO SPRUCE AND BALSAM,
CUT-OVER AREAS, KAPUSKASING DISTRICT, 1935–8

Site	Location	Number of quadrats	Spruce	Balsam	Spruce or balsam
		1938 survey			
I–P	Strip	117	56	90	92
I–P	Road	30	50	70	77
I–M	Strip	236	44	89	91
I–M	Road	65	55	94	95
II–A	Strip	107	76	90	93
II–A	Road	40	80	77	92
II–B	Strip	66	89	47	94
II–B	Road	20	95	45	95
II–C	Strip	24	58	50	63
II–C	Road	8	100	25	100
II–D	Strip	136	81	77	90
II–D	Road	48	85	75	94
III	Strip	15	100	0	100
III	Road	4	100	0	100
		Average of 1935, 1936, 1937, and 1938 surveys			
I–P	Strip	646	52	80	86
I–P	Road	197	49	65	76
I–M	Strip	649	40	84	88
I–M	Road	173	46	79	85
II–A	Strip	535	76	88	94
II–A	Road	191	71	74	89
II–B	Strip	572	91	47	43
II–B	Road	248	90	39	35
II–C	Strip	113	77	46	82
II–C	Road	51	88	33	90
II–D	Strip	577	79	66	90
II–D	Road	171	77	56	87
III	Strip	32	100	9	100
III	Road	10	90	0	90

3. REGENERATION ON CUT-OVER AREAS, 1940: *E. Bonner*

Purpose

A resurvey of portions of cutover surveyed in 1933 and in 1935 and a comparative survey of areas cut to four-foot wood and to sixteen-foot wood.

The sixteen-foot wood was "hand bunched," a method of logging no longer in use. The data do not apply to sixteen-foot skidded operations.

Results

1. In Table 3 of the report the stand per acre at two different ages after cutting is shown for an area of 1928–9 cutover.

Site	Location	Total spruce		Total balsam	
		1933–5	1939	1933–5	1939
I—P	Strip	1437	1050	22880	13500
I—P	Road	1762	1200	20671	10020
I—M	Strip	1898	2700	31121	13000
II—A	Strip	2457	1582	17335	14600
II—A	Road	3128	943	15244	4541
II—B	Strip	5506	6139	7197	4720
II—B	Road	5737	1998	14004	2398
II—D	Strip	4723	3858	5815	9571

Table 4 of the report shows the stocking record for the same area and same ages after cutting.

Site	Location	Spruce		Balsam	
		1935	1939	1935	1939
I—P	Strip	95	72	100	91
I—P	Road	67	69	100	77
I—M	Strip	61	67	94	100
I—M	Road	56	75	56	100
II—A	Strip	89	80	94	90
II—A	Road	68	73	82	67
II—B	Strip	98	97	43	60
II—B	Road	89	90	45	49
II—D	Strip	75	91	73	83
II—D	Road	81	91	75	82
III	Strip	100	100	0	4
III	Road	75	100	0	17

It is pointed out that the regeneration on the area is very satisfactory and the figures in the above two tables support that statement. It is also pointed out that cutting was carried out during and after a very good seed year for spruce and that the regeneration is therefore above average.

On the basis of stand per acre, on all sites except where there was dense alder growth, spruce improved its position at the expense of balsam.

For the majority of the types the degree of stocking increased although in many cases the change was too small to have much significance. It is concluded that the major changes occur in the clumps of spruce or balsam rather than among the solitary individuals and that therefore the stocking is not appreciably altered during the years following cutting.

2. In the comparison of areas cut to four-foot and to sixteen-foot wood the findings are:

(i) Better stands of spruce in the areas cut to four-foot wood.

(ii) On all sites (except the I–M which was practically without spruce regeneration and declared untypical) the regeneration was better on the area cut to four-foot wood where there was an increase in both advance growth and in seedlings.

(iii) The degree of stocking of merchantable trees only for mature timbered areas is given as follows (see Table 10 of the report). (Figures are percentages of 1/600-acre quadrats.)

Site	Spruce	Balsam	Spruce or balsam	Number of quadrats
Softwood slope	37	27	58	216
Mixedwood	16	16	28	102
Softwood flat	65	2	65	57
Swamp	46	6	50	319

4. Table 12 of the report shows the stocking of spruce and balsam, compiled from the results of the surveys made in five-year old cutovers since 1933. (Figures are percentages of 1/600-acre quadrats.)

Site	Location	Spruce	Balsam	Spruce or balsam	Number of quadrats
I—P	Strip	49	79	84	723
I—P	Road	47	63	74	219
I—M	Strip	36	84	87	829
I—M	Road	46	79	85	214
II—A	Strip	73	86	93	596
II—A	Road	68	76	89	224
II—B	Strip	89	50	93	688
II—B	Road	91	43	94	297
II—C	Strip	70	45	76	155
II—C	Road	87	39	90	84
II—D	Strip	76	67	90	677
II—D	Road	76	59	89	221
III	Strip	100	9	100	32
III	Road	90	0	90	10
Weighted average		65	69	88	Total 4969

Conclusions

1. All types are well stocked to either spruce or balsam.

2. On Site I the entire dependence is on balsam for 41 per cent of the area.

3. In the case of spruce, the average of all types shows 49 per cent of the area stocked with seedlings and 46 per cent with advance growth; 16 per cent of the area is entirely dependent on advance growth. The figures for balsam are very similar (55, 49, and 14). Thus dependence is on advance growth for the stocking of approximately 15 per cent of the area.

4. For spruce on all sites and balsam on most sites, areas cut during good seed years are better stocked than areas cut during poor seed years. The difference is, on the average, approximately 10 per cent.

[The results obtained by this survey reveal a more favourable condition of spruce regeneration than is to be found in any of the other Company surveys.

The 1945, 1946, and 1949 surveys reviewed in the succeeding pages reveal a less favourable condition with regard to spruce on the slopes.]

4. REGENERATION STUDIES, 1945: *R. C. Hosie*

Purpose

Primarily to determine whether or not, under present cutting methods, the uplands are being adequately restocked to spruce, and if they are not what steps should be taken to assure a future spruce cut on these lands.

The study was carried out in uncut stands and cut-over areas on the timber limits of the Company near Kapuskasing.

Method

The line plot method with quadrats of 1/600 acre, as developed and used by the Company, supplemented by observations over a wide range of conditions.

Results

1. In the uncut slope type (I—P and I—M) the stocking of spruce is about 50 per cent and that of balsam fir nearly 100. Spruce stocking is slightly higher in the pure conifer stands than in the mixedwood stands but there is no noticeable difference for balsam. Spruce averages 2000 stems to the acre, balsam fir 18,000. The highest numbers per acre for spruce occur in the pure conifer stands.

2. In the cut slope type the stocking of spruce is considerably less than 50 per cent and that of balsam fir below 88 per cent. The number per acre for spruce ranges from 500 to 1200 and for balsam fir is less than 6,500.

3. The regeneration of spruce and balsam fir on the slope types is practically at an end once the overhead stand is cut and the young conifer crop now on a cut-over area was practically all there before the cutting was made.

4. The effect of logging is to reduce the regeneration figures by approximately one-half.

5. To ensure a future cut of spruce equivalent to that now being logged from the slopes it is recommended that the roads on such cut-over areas be planted to spruce as soon after hauling as possible.

5. REGENERATION STUDIES, 1946: *R. C. Hosie*

Purpose

A check on the results of the survey made on the limits of the Company in 1945; consideration of the possibilities of planting trees effectively under bush conditions; and the selection of a site suitable for a forest tree nursery.

Method

The work was largely in the nature of a reconnaisance, sponsored jointly by the Department of Lands and Forests and the Spruce Falls Power and Paper Company. Ten days were spent on the limits of the Longlac Pulp and Paper Company and approximately six weeks in the Kapuskasing-Hearst area. Mr. E. Bonner, of the Spruce Falls Power and Paper Company, assisted in all phases of the work.

Results

These are presented under the headings, Composition, Regeneration, Logging, and Planting.

Under "Composition" it is stated that on the slopes, particularly on clay soils, there are sizeable tracts that have neither spruce nor balsam on them at present. It is also stated that on many of these there is no possibility of seeding-in as there are no seed trees, and that even where seed trees are present there is no apparent increase in the quantity of spruce.

Under "Regeneration" some of the difficulties encountered by the field worker in deciding on the age of seedlings are discussed and it is pointed out that very often so-called reproduction since logging is actually advance growth.

Under "Logging" reference is made to the areas where some form of selection logging had been practised and it is stated that such logging did not encourage seeding-in of spruce but may even tend to discourage it.

Under "Planting" some of the tools that might possibly be used are described and reference is made to the best time to undertake planting.

The conclusions reached are essentially the same as those stated in the 1945 report (No. 4): that the cut-over slope areas are not adequately stocked to spruce and are not seeding in to spruce, and are therefore not going to produce a satisfactory volume of spruce in the next cut unless given some assistance. The assistance advocated is the planting of spruce on the roads soon after hauling.

The report concludes with a diary of the trips made by the author.

6. REGENERATION SURVEYS, 1949: *E. Bonner*

Purpose

To determine the regeneration on burned cutover, on twenty-year-old cutover, and in mature stands and to classify the burned cutover on the basis of planting possibilities.

Results

1. The percentage of 1/600-acre quadrats stocked on burned cutover is:

Site	Number of quadrats	Spruce	Balsam	Spruce or Balsam
I	1625	6	4	10
II (flat)	605	56	2	56
II (swamp)	421	32	17	35
III (semi-muskeg)	13	92	0	92

2. The percentage of 1/600-acre quadrats stocked in twenty-year-old cutover is as follows (figures in brackets are the values based on a 1/1000 acre quadrat).

Site	Number of quadrats	Spruce	Balsam	Spruce or balsam
I—P	305	55 (38)	77 (59)	86
I—M	1023	34 (22)	70 (51)	80
II—A	1168	61 (43)	86 (69)	93
II—B	1040	93 (80)	58 (41)	99
II—C	22	100	36	100
II—D	904	69 (50)	78 (60)	94
III	59	98	7	98

3. Changes in stocking and in numbers per acre of regeneration with increasing age of cutover were noted. A table of stocking percentages and three graphs in the report indicate that

(a) On Site I (high ground) the numbers per acre of balsam decrease very rapidly during the first twenty years after cutting. The numbers of spruce also decease but at a much slower rate. The degree of stocking to balsam decreases, that of spruce increases slightly.

(b) On Site II (flat) stocking of spruce is high and steadily increasing and that of balsam is rising sharply. There is apparently some seeding-in of spruce as the numbers per acre are gradually increasing.

(c) On Site II (swamp) the numbers per acre of both spruce and balsam are decreasing. The stocking to spruce is decreasing and that to balsam increasing. However, the stocking to spruce is still over 60 per cent.

4. The percentage of 1/600-acre quadrats stocked to merchantable trees in mature timber is:

Type	Number of quadrats	Spruce	Balsam	Spruce or balsam
Softwood slope	704	30	25	50
Mixedwood	137	13	25	35
Softwood flat	103	46	8	52
Swamp	584	33	14	42

These percentages are low compared to those obtained in five-, ten-, fifteen-, and twenty-year cutovers, but it is pointed out that as yet no data are available to indicate what minimum stocking is required at twenty years to guarantee an average cordage at maturity.

[The thought expressed in the above paragraph reveals one of the problems in connection with forest regeneration that has not yet been solved: the degree of stocking at different ages following cutting necessary to provide full stocking at maturity.]